How to Use a Short Sale

to Stop Home Foreclosure

and Protect Your Finances

Other McGraw-Hill Books by Robert Irwin

How to Use a Short Sale to Stop Home Foreclosure and Protect Your Finances

ROBERT IRWIN

New York Chicago San Francisco Lisbon London Madrid Mexico City
Milan New Delhi San Juan Seoul Singapore Sydney Toronto

The McGraw·Hill Companies

Library of Congress Cataloging-in-Publication Data
Irwin, Robert.
  How to use a short sale to stop home foreclosure and protect your finances / by Robert Irwin.
     p.   cm.
  ISBN 0-07-163558-0 (alk. paper)
    1. House selling—United States. 2. Foreclosure—United States. 3. Mortgage loans—United States. I. Title.
  HD259.I787 2009
  33.33'83—dc22
                                                                          2009011290

1 2 3 4 5 6 7 8 9 0   FGR/FGR   0 1 3 2 1 0 9

ISBN: 978-0-07-163558-5
MHID: 0-07-163558-0

This publication is designed to provide accurate and authoritative information in regard to the subject matter covered. It is sold with the understanding that neither the author nor the publisher is engaged in rendering legal, accounting, futures/securities trading, tax, or other professional service. If legal advice or other expert assistance is required, the services of a competent professional person should be sought.

—From a Declaration of Principles jointly adopted
by a Committee of the American Bar
Association and a Committee of Publishers

AUTHOR'S NOTE: The information provided in this book is intended to be helpful in charting a course through the troubled waters of foreclosure and short sales. However, every borrower's situation is unique. Before attempting a short sale or making any financial decision, you are advised to seek the counsel of a competent real estate attorney and accountant.

The term Realtor® is a registered collective membership mark that identifies a real estate professional who is a member of the National Association of Realtors®.
"MLS.com America's Real Estate Portal" is a servicemark of MLS Network, Inc.

McGraw-Hill books are available at special quantity discounts to use as premiums and sales promotions, or for use in corporate training programs. To contact a representative please visit the Contact Us pages at www.mhprofessional.com.

This book is printed on acid-free paper.

For Nicole and Marc, and Heather and Jason.

Contents

Preface

When I proposed a book on real estate short sales to be written for sellers and their agents (and that would be helpful for buyers as well), my editor jumped at the idea. Originally I called it *How to Sell a Home When You Owe More Than It's Worth*. (The current title was deemed more descriptive.) We both felt that there was a great need to help people who were facing foreclosure, who were under water, who couldn't keep up with their mortgages, who really wanted a good alternative to having to walk away from their homes.

This book is the result.

It's designed to show you how a short sale can salvage credit and peace of mind. It reveals how short sales work by offering many examples of successful sellers. It provides the essential elements of a package that you need to give a lender in order to facilitate the sale. It explains an authorization letter (and gives a sample) that will allow the lender to talk to an agent, an attorney, and others. And it provides help in determining how to find a good agent and to calculate whether or not you, as a seller, actually need a short sale. It gives you net sheets to help prove to a lender that a short sale will save it not only time but also money and that the lender should move forward with the transaction.

There are chapters devoted to getting a loan modification, to finding and dealing with a loss mitigation committee, and how to complete the deal.

It also exposes many of the scams that are facing those who are involved in short sales, the potential problem when the Internal Revenue Service deems the short sale discount to be taxable income to the seller (and legal ways around it), and how to beat the deadlines that can doom a short sale.

In short, this book has all the information you're likely to need to successfully complete a short sale.

Robert Irwin
www.robertirwin.com

How to Use a Short Sale

to Stop Home Foreclosure

and Protect Your Finances

How a Short Sale Works

A real estate broker once told me, "Short sales aren't hard to put through—they're impossible!"

She was, of course, reflecting only her own poor experiences with them. Since then I've talked with brokers who specialize only in short sales and claim a success rate of from 30 to as high as 90 percent. And I've met individual sellers who have successfully handled their own short sales. All of which is to say that while the common perception is that short sales are very difficult, if you know what you're doing, they can be quick and relatively easy.

What Is a Short Sale?

When you sell your home (whether directly or through an agent) for less than the balance you owe on your mortgage(s), it is called a *short sale* or sometimes a *short payoff*. Many lenders are willing to accept a short payoff (less than they are owed) when the owner cannot make the mortgage payments. The reason a lender will forgive all or a large portion of the unpaid amount of the loan is that a short sale saves it time and money by avoiding a more costly foreclosure procedure.

For example, you bought your property for $200,000, putting nothing down; hence you borrowed $200,000. But, the collapse of the real estate market means that the value of your home has plunged. Today it's worth only $150,000. That means that you're upside down (under water) to the tune of $50,000. That's how much more you owe on your mortgage than the value of your home.

Now a triggering event occurs. For example, your mortgage resets to a much higher interest rate and monthly payment, which you cannot afford. Because you owe $200,000 and your house is worth only $150,000, you have negative equity. This precludes you from being able to refinance (no lender will offer you a mortgage when you owe so much more than your property's value), and you can't sell in the traditional manner (unless you come up with $50,000 out of your own pocket—something I've yet to see a seller willing and able to do!).

You stop making payments, and you face foreclosure. You can't refi, and you can't sell (in the usual way). What can you do?

One good alternative is to get the lender to accept less than you owe; in this case, instead of $200,000, only $150,000. If you can get your lender to accept $50,000 less (plus transaction costs), you can still sell your home—and without spending a dime of your money.

That's the big trick, of course. Getting the lender to take less. When you're successful, it's called a short sale.

CAUTION

Short sales can be complex transactions. Be sure that you consult an attorney and accountant for legal and tax advice before proceeding with one.

Who Needs a Short Sale?

In a difficult real estate market, short sales can be a positive force, especially when you're facing foreclosure. They are extremely useful and can do the following.

What a Short Sale Can Do for a Seller

Here's what a short sale can do for a seller:

- **Allow you to sell when you're "under water."** (In some areas as many as a quarter of all homeowners owe more than their homes are worth.)
- **Avoid or stop foreclosure.** (It's a *short* sale—the foreclosure process ends the moment you no longer own the property.)
- **Preserve your credit.** (There's almost nothing worse on a credit report than a foreclosure. The short sale prevents it.)
- **Safeguard your finances.** (This will stop you drawing down your reserves by making payments you can't afford.)

Many millions of homeowners are facing foreclosure as this is written, and many more are likely to join their ranks. Figure 1.1 shows where most of these foreclosures are coming from. Do you find yourself there?

How a Short Sale Works

The following are several examples of how a short sale has worked to help sellers.

Note: While the examples in this book are taken from real life, because of their financial circumstances, the people mentioned

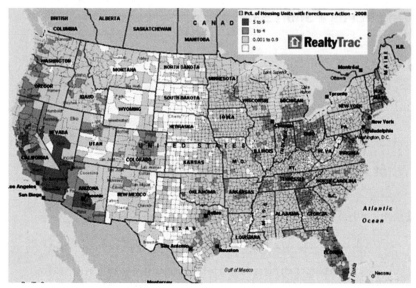

Figure 1.1 Foreclosures by state and major metropolitan areas in 2008. Data Source: RealtyTrac Inc.

have requested anonymity, and hence their names and some of their circumstances have been changed.

The Liar's Loan

Peta was recently divorced and was now supporting four children all under the age of nine. She worked as a waitress in a coffee shop, and her income, with tips, was under $36,000 a year. She owned a very small two-bedroom, one-bath house that she had earlier bought with her husband. She desperately wanted to move into a bigger place, preferably a house of her own.

One day she was at work in the coffee shop when she met a businessman who struck up a conversation with her. Stan said he was a real estate investor. She spilled her story out to him, and he seemed sympathetic. Stan said he had a home that he wanted to get rid of that would be perfect for her. It was on a bluff with a beautiful view of the mountains, it was more than 3,000 square feet in size, and it was in great condition. He said they might be able to help each other out. It all depended on her credit. Did she have good credit?

Peta's parents had emphasized the importance of always paying back debts. She had worked hard to maintain excellent credit, even paying off all the debts her husband incurred before the divorce. She had several credits cards, and since she usually paid cash, the amounts owed on them was very low. She had also borrowed to buy a used car and meticulously made her payments on time. And though it was difficult, the house payments were made promptly every month. She said her credit was excellent.

Stan smiled and said, "Good, good, that will work." Then he drove her to the property and showed her the house where he was living. It was huge with all the modern amenities including three bathrooms and had a bedroom for each of her children. It was, indeed, perfect.

Then Stan told her that the price of the home was $700,000. He said that the house used to be worth a lot more, but the market had turned soft (it was in 2007) and that the fair market price was down a bit. Plus, there just weren't any buyers out there for that price.

Peta was a stunned by the price. Certainly she'd love to move into such a beautiful big home in such a nice location. But, she couldn't imagine that she could afford the place, not on her meager income.

Stan, the real estate investor, told her not to worry; he said he'd handle everything.

Stan said that all that he needed from her was a commitment to buy the place. She didn't need to be concerned about the payments. He just needed someone to buy and get a new loan so he could get his own money out. He realized that the payments would be high, so he'd take care of them. He'd said he'd make her payments for the first two years. And he'd also handle the down payment (there wasn't any because he was getting a 100 percent loan) as well as the closing costs. It wouldn't cost her a dime to move in.

On the day the deal closed, he'd said he'd even give her $25,000 in cash to help her get started!

Stan came in for lunch about every other day from then on and kept talking about the deal. Peta was tempted, but she wasn't sure. She couldn't put her finger on it, but something didn't seem right. When she mentioned it to her friends, most of them also were wary. One said, "Peta, it's just too good to really be true!"

However, Peta couldn't see how she could lose. So, after several weeks, she agreed to move forward on the deal with Stan. He seemed very happy about it and had her fill out a purchase agreement with the price of $700,000 with an interest-only loan for 100 percent of LTV (loan-to-value).

The purchase was actually made using a "no doc" loan. (This is also sometimes called a "liar's loan.") All Peta had to do was to fill out a fairly short application giving her personal information—her name, address, place of employment, and so on. Stan filled in the portion about her income and assets. Nothing was verified.

The lender's broker didn't seem too inquisitive. (After all, he was pulling a big commission on the deal). The lender did eventually verify her employment and did pull a credit report on her. Her credit was impeccable, as she had said, and her credit score was above 700. Perfect for the deal.

Stan reported progress to her almost daily and said that the deal was moving along beautifully. Then one bright morning in September, he drove her to a title insurance company where she filled out a mass of paperwork for the mortgage. The next day he came into the coffee shop with the key and gave it to her, telling her the house was hers.

She drove her kids and herself to the home after work that evening. Stan had moved out and had left the place a mess. There were half-empty boxes strewn everywhere, and the paint on the walls in lots of spots was nicked. There were spots on the carpet she hadn't seen before. But she didn't care. The house was hers. She moved in immediately.

I'm sure, dear reader, that you are thinking that this story can't have a happy ending. If you're thinking that, you're only partly correct. Read on.

Peta lived in the home for almost five months before she got wind of anything being wrong. It was a registered letter to her notifying her that the mortgage payment hadn't been made for the past three months.

Peta immediately tried to contact Stan. But that was proving difficult. She had wanted to talk to him about the $25,000 he had promised her when she moved in but never delivered.

The trouble was that once Stan moved out of the house, she couldn't find him. He didn't have a forwarding address. And he never came by the restaurant anymore.

The next month another registered letter arrived informing Peta that unless she paid four months of mortgage payments immediately, the lender would put the home into foreclosure. The payments were $4,089 a month, not including taxes and insurance. She owed $16,350 immediately. That was almost half of her entire annual income.

One of Peta's coworkers was dating an attorney, and the woman arranged for Peta to meet with him on a pro bono basis. Peta explained the situation and said there was, of course, no way the woman could make the payments. He speculated that Stan had probably not been able to sell the house legitimately for that price. So instead, he had suckered her into a phony deal, perhaps in collusion with the lender's broker, who got a fat fee. He had taken the money from the mortgage, made a couple of payments to throw the lender off track, and had hightailed it out of town. The attorney said he'd look into it, but he doubted that he'd find Stan.

In the meantime, the house was in Peta's name; she owed the money on the mortgage, including the back payments. If she didn't pay, the lender would foreclose and at the least she'd lose her good credit rating. At the worst, the bank might find reason to prosecute her for fraud. The attorney told her that the best thing to do was to quickly sell and pay off the mortgage. That should resolve the problem.

Peta contacted an agent that afternoon but quickly learned that prices were falling. Her $700,000 house was now worth only $600,000. After commission and closing costs were thrown in, her "net" would only be about $560,000. That was $140,000 less than she owed on her mortgage. (Remember, it was 100 percent of the purchase price loan.) She'd have to come up with $140,000 just to sell the house!

Peta said that she had only about $2,000 saved in the bank.

The agent said there was another way. A short sale. He would try to find a buyer for the house at the current market value. And then he would try to get the lender to accept a short payoff—take less than what was owed.

Peta began to cry with relief. The agent told her not to celebrate yet. They had to find a buyer. And then they had to convince the lender.

Peta went home feeling much better. There she found another registered letter from the lender informing here that it had filed a *notice of default* beginning the foreclosure action. She had roughly three months to make up all back payments or lose the home and essentially have her credit ruined. (A foreclosure typically will stay on a credit report for from 7 to 10 years.)

The next month Peta moved back into her old, small home. She had kept it and rented it out; now she told the tenants they had to move. They grumbled but complied.

Then things picked up. The agent found a buyer who agreed to purchase for $600,000—the market price. Peta signed the sales agreement. The agent, it turned out was very much on top of things. He immediately prepared a lender's package which included a hardship letter. In it Peta explained that she was divorced and that her income was only about $3,000 a month. She included pay stubs and bank statements to prove that she didn't have the income or assets to make the mortgage payments. The agent also included a comparison sheet showing how much the lender would lose if it allowed the property to be sold at a later foreclosure auction in a market where prices were falling as opposed to accepting an immediate short payoff. (The loss was significantly higher with waiting to go to foreclosure.)

Unfortunately, the lender dragged its feet. And time marched on ever closer to Peta's deadline for a foreclosure auction that would take the property away from her and virtually destroy her credit.

Then one day the agent called and said the lender agreed. The buyer still wanted the house. She had to come down immediately and sign the papers.

Peta did, and the next day the house was history. She celebrated by taking her four children out for ice cream. Her relief was palpable, and she slept well for the first time in months.

Unfortunately, the story isn't quite over. As part of the short sale agreement, the lender demanded that Peta pay back something, in this case $5,000 in the form of a promissory note payable at $50 per month plus interest until paid. And there was the chance that the Internal Revenue Service (IRS) could get involved. It could see the money forgiven by the lender, in this case $140,000, as income, in which case Peta would owe taxes on it! (An accountant told her not to worry because a new law had been passed which would probably eliminate this threat—see Chapter 10.)

Nevertheless, Peta considered herself lucky to get out of the deal only partially scathed. (The missed payments did put a nick on her credit, and she did owe $50 a month back to the lender.) But, it was a lesson well learned.

MORAL Obviously, when something is too good to be true, it usually is. Keep in mind, however, that Peta's short sale enabled her to avoid a foreclosure, although a number of late payments were recorded. She didn't get prosecuted for what was a very sketchy deal. And she did have to pay back some money, although at a rate she could afford.

If you were thinking that Peta's story was unusual or even unique, you'd be wrong. Almost every broker I talked with who handled short sales had some version of it to relay. Apparently this kind of hokeypokey was rampant as the real estate bubble was bursting and prices were collapsing.

The Subprime Lost Opportunity

Suvi and Chad were raising a family in Los Angeles and renting a small house. They had two children, and they desperately wanted to move to a better neighborhood, hopefully into their own home.

Real estate was booming at the time, and everyone said that all you had to do was buy a house, any house, and in a few years you'd be rich. It seemed like a good idea. After all, they were repeatedly told that real estate prices only went up.

So they contacted a real estate agent who told them that, yes, he could probably get them into a decent home in a good neighborhood. But they'd have to move swiftly since prices were moving upward at a very fast pace.

The agent, Castro, showed them at least a dozen different houses, many of which seemed adequate. Suvi felt that one, however, was really perfect. It had three bedrooms and two baths, and it had a living room, dining room, and family room. Best of all it was in a good neighborhood with good schools. They told Castro that they wanted the property.

He said that he'd write up an offer, but first he called a mortgage broker friend of his, Angel, who came right over; she took their information. Suvi worked in a clothing shop as a seam-stress, and Chad was a gardener. Between them their income was about $2,500 a month. Despite this limited income, they were both very industrious, and over the years they had saved almost $13,000.

After they filled out an application, the mortgage broker, Angel, ran a credit check and found that they had missed a few payments here and there. And a few years earlier their car had been repossessed when Chad was out of work. Their credit score was in the 500s.

Angel said that it was too low for them to qualify for an "A" mortgage (a loan conforming to major underwriting standards that offered the best rates and terms) but that they could get a "subprime" mortgage. This meant that the interest rate would be higher and that there were more costs ("points") to pay, but it would allow them to acquire the property.

The house was priced at $250,000. They could get a 100 percent subprime loan on it, but the interest rate would be 8 percent. The mortgage and interest came to $1,667 a month plus taxes and insurance.

Suvi looked at Chad, and he seemed as shocked as she was. "No way!" he said. Their total income was only $2,500 a month. That would amount to two-thirds of it. They had food to buy and cloth-ing and insurance and medical and everything else that a family needs to live on.

"Not to worry," Angel said. "We can put you into an ARM [adjustable rate mortgage]. The interest rate for the first three years will be fixed at 3.5 percent, and your payments will only be $730 a month. You can afford that, can't you?"

Suvi and Chad nodded. It would be tight, but that was afford-able. "But," Suvi asked, "What happens after three years?"

The mortgage broker, Angel, smiled and said, "The mortgage resets. It goes back to 8 percent."

"Do our payments then rise to the $1,667 a month?" Suvi continued.

"Yes," Angel responded, "But don't be too concerned. When that happens, you should be able to refinance and get another mortgage with low payments all over again. You can keep doing it over and over and keep your payments low."

Suvi and Chad nodded. It was amazing what miracles could be performed in the modern world of finance.

They went back to Castro, the agent, who prepared an offer. The deal was made, and a month later they signed the loan documents to get the house. When they signed, Angel pointed out that there was negative amortization on the loan. This meant that interest not paid during the initial three-year "teaser" period would be added to the loan amount. At the end of the three years they'd owe roughly $280,000 instead of the original amount of $250,000. But that shouldn't be a worry, she continued, what with the way prices of property were moving up.

Angel further informed them that there were "points" to the loan. One point was equal to 1 percent of the loan amount. Four points on the loan came to $10,000. Plus there was $3,500 in closing costs. All were payable in cash.

Suvi looked at Chad who shook his head. He didn't understand, and she wasn't sure she did either. But, they had nearly all the needed cash in the bank. The papers were in front of them, and all they had to do was sign and they had their new home. So they signed.

After hearing about the subprime mess that hit the mortgage industry in 2007 and 2008, I'm sure many readers are shaking their heads. Those poor kids were in trouble. And indeed they were.

Suvi and Chad moved into their new home, fixed it up just the way they liked it, and never missed a payment. For three years things went well until one day they received a letter from their lender notifying them that their monthly payments were resetting from $730 a month to a new payment of $1,667. The lender cautioned them that to keep their credit rating, they needed to make the new payments on time.

Immediately Suvi called Angel, the mortgage broker and went to see her with Chad. When they explained the situation, Angel shook her head sadly. "The market has collapsed. Your home is probably only worth $200,000 today. But, you owe $280,000 and with financing fees you'd need a new loan of at least $290,000. There's no way you can refinance. I'm sorry. You'll just have to make the new payments and hope the market eventually turns around."

Suvi and Chad's income hadn't appreciably increased. There was no way they could make the new payments. So they went back to see their original real estate agent, Castro, from whom they bought the house.

Castro said that their only real alternative was to sell. That way they could at least preserve their credit and eventually buy another home. But the market value of the house was now only around $200,000. That was $80,000 less than they owed. They'd have to come up with $80,000, plus his commission and closing costs, just to sell.

Suvi almost cried, and Chad became angry. The $80,000 was, of course, impossible.

"The only other thing we can try," Castro said, "is a short sale. We can sell the property for $200,000 and try to get the lender to accept a short payoff—less than what is owed. But, I have to tell you that I've had little luck with these."

Chad said, "Try." Suvi nodded.

It took seven months before a buyer appeared who made an offer for the property. During that time Suvi and Chad had tried to make partial payments on the mortgage, but their checks had been returned. The lender wanted full payment or none at all. Now they were in default. And time was running out. The lender was threatening to sell their home "on the courthouse steps" in about 60 days.

Castro said he immediately sent the buyer's offer and short sale proposal to the lender. Then they waited. After a month, the lender's loss mitigation committee replied saying it needed more information. It needed to know why Suvi and Chad couldn't make their payments. It also needed documentation to show their income and assets. And it needed to know why it should accept a shorter payoff—why that was more advantageous to it than simply letting the house go into foreclosure.

Castro had Suvi and Chad write a heartwarming hardship letter about their financial situation. He had them include pay stubs and bank deposit records. (They had only about $500 in the bank, having used their other funds to fix up the house.) And Castro included a sheet comparing what the lender would get on a short payoff compared to a foreclosure. (The lender got significantly more on the short payoff.) He mailed in all the information.

After a few more weeks the lender notified Castro that it was authorizing a BPO (broker's price opinion). It would pay a local broker to give an opinion as to the value of the property.

A few more weeks went by. Then the lender called Castro and told him that it would agree to the short sale. Documents would follow shortly. Unfortunately, on the same day Suvi and Chad received a certified letter telling them that their house would be auctioned off at foreclosure within three weeks. Time was running out.

They immediately called Castro who immediately tried calling the lender. However, by then, the lender literally had tens of thousands of foreclosures working and almost as many appeals for short sales. Castro simply couldn't get through to anyone.

After a couple of weeks Castro did get through to a loss mediation representative who said he'd call off the foreclosure proceedings until the lender had time to do the paperwork to conclude the short sale. Castro immediately called Suvi and Chad who celebrated with a rare dinner out.

A week later their house was sold "on the courthouse" steps. An eviction notice came shortly afterward, and they were forced to leave their home. Apparently the lender's legal department never got the word from its loss mitigation committee, and the foreclosure progressed to its normal conclusion.

In a breakdown of monumental proportions such as the recent mortgage mess, often a lender's right hand doesn't know what its left hand is doing. Furthermore, although the vast majority of mortgage brokers do their best to explain the terms and dangers of the mortgage they are selling, some do not. And all too frequently, especially in the area of subprimes, the borrowers simply don't understand the nature of the mortgage or the risks involved.

The Option Payment ARM Debacle

Our next example concerns the option payment ARM or as it has come to be called, the "option ARM." It's of particular interest because this type of mortgage is just starting to reset (going to a higher interest rate and payment) as this is written and will continue to reset into 2011. In other words, there are lots of people out there who are facing this problem. (See Figure 1.2.)

Sybille had a good-paying job and was generally happy with her career. She was an architect in a small independent office that specialized in designing commercial buildings. The projects were big, the money was good, and the work was rewarding. Her bank account was in the low six figures. She had put thoughts of marriage and a family off into the future.

During the real estate boom of the early part of the first decade of the twenty-first century, she watched as friends and associates bought properties and made killings on them. Everyone, it seemed, was making spectacular money on real estate.

So she decided to dive in. She knew a good real estate broker and told him to get her "invested up." Clarence, the broker, knew

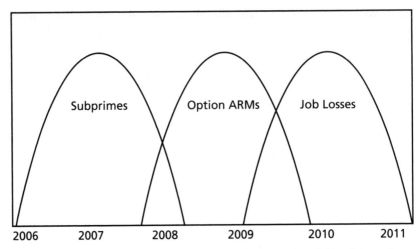

Figure 1.2 Waves of foreclosure: There are three waves of foreclosure that began with the bursting of the real estate bubble. The first wave was caused by subprime foreclosures. The second by alt-A (stated income/assets loans) and option ARM foreclosures, and the third by mortgagors who had lost their jobs, and subsequently lost their homes. Chart projected to 2011.

a good fish when he saw one and immediately put her into five separate properties. He asked, "Do you want to maximize your profits?"

"Certainly," she replied. So he explained, "The real way to make money in real estate, or anything else for that matter, is to leverage your investments. You can make some money on one property, but you'll make five times as much on five properties. And the less you personally put in, the greater your leverage."

Each property had its own mortgage, but all of them were with the same lender. In order to maximize the leverage, Clarence explained, he got option ARMs. These were loans where essentially she could decide how much she wanted to pay each month. For example, the loans were all at 6 percent, a very good rate for the time. They averaged $400,000 a property. If she made the regular amortized payment on each, it would be roughly $2,400 a month plus taxes and insurance. However, if she chose the lowest payment option, it was only $800 a month, the other roughly $1,700 being added to the mortgage amount in the form of negative amortization. (In theory she could skip a month, and the entire interest payment would be added to the mortgage, but her broker, Clarence, suggested that this would be a bad idea because it might make the lender wary. "Just make the minimum payment. You'll be selling the houses for a fortune in a year, anyhow," he said.)

Sybille put 5 percent, or $20,000, down per house for a total investment of $100,000. Once the houses were bought, Clarence quickly rented them, and, even after property management fees, together they brought in close to $1,000 a month in profits. Sybille was making 12 percent on her investment and figured to double or even triple it in a year or so when property prices went up. (After all, she only put $20,000 down on each property. If they went up by $20,000 in price, or just 5 percent, she'd double her investment.) It was so easy. She never dreamed that making money could be like falling off a log.

Well, dear reader, I'm sure you're anticipating the comeuppance of this story. It can't be that easy. It wasn't.

Shortly after Sybille bought the properties, the price of real estate staggered, then began falling. Instead of going up by 5 percent, the prices went down by 5 percent. Then 10 percent. Then 30 percent. Her $400,000 properties were suddenly only worth $280,000 or less apiece She was upside down by roughly $100,000 a property, or half a million on all five.

However, Clarence her broker wasn't worried, and hence, neither was Sybille. Clarence pointed out that all five were still rented. Indeed, a shortage of good rental housing had occurred, and now she was clearing nearly $1,200 a month on all five together, or $14,400 a year—a 14 percent return on her original $100,000 investment. What could be so bad?

The whole investment strategy fell off a cliff when, after three years with the market still not reaching a bottom, the original low interest rate on her five loans ended and the mortgages on all five properties reset to $2,400 a month apiece, or roughly three times her previous payment. Suddenly, in the course of one month, she went from a positive cash flow of $1,200 to a negative cash flow of $6,800 a month. She had to take $6,800 a month out of her pocket just to make the monthly payments. That was almost as much as her total income each month!

Sybille immediately called Clarence who said he had just gotten off the phone with another client with a similar problem. Clarence said, "Just hold tight. Make the payments. We've never had a market that stayed down like this. It'll be a V curve. It'll drop down and spring right back up. Just hold on, and things will be fine."

Sybille held on for a year going through all the rest of her savings. When she was finally broke, she called Clarence and said, "You've got to do something. I can't afford to make one more payment."

Clarence gave her more bad news. Her properties were now worth only $250,000 apiece. That meant that on average she owed $130,000 more on each one than it was worth. She was under water to the tune of $650,000 on all five.

Sybille dropped the phone. When she picked it back up, she was angry. She berated Clarence for deceiving her about the market. He protested, saying that no one could have foreseen such a catastrophic collapse. She yelled at him for getting her into such high-leverage financing. He again protested, pointing out that she wanted to maximize her investment. High leverage worked both ways—it produced greater profits in good times and greater losses in bad.

He said that if she simply stopped making payments and "walked" away from the properties, her credit would be ruined for as long as a decade. She wouldn't be able to buy another home, let alone get a car loan or credit cards. And the lender might come after her and sue her for a deficiency judgment, forcing her to pay for any money it lost on foreclosing.

In the end, Sybille asked if there was anything she could do. Clarence replied that the only way out was a short sale, getting the lender to take less than it was owed. A short payoff.

"Can you do it?" she asked. "Maybe," Clarence replied.

He put all five properties up for sale at just below market price, advertising them as short sales. He explained that to sell, the lender would have to take the difference between what was owed and the market price *minus* his commission and closing costs. (After all, Sybille had no money to pay commission and closing costs.) The lender's loss would be something like $150,000 per property, or $750,000 total. "The lender will never do that," Sybille exclaimed. "We'll see," Clarence replied.

At their low price, given the amount they could be rented for, the properties actually made attractive investments. Clarence found a buyer for all five in less than two months. He had Sybille sign a sales agreement and proposal to the lender. Then he told her, "You have to make a good case that you can't continue making the payments. After all, you've made the payments for a year after the loan reset. Now, suddenly you've stopped. The lender will want to know why. You have to explain you have no more assets and that you don't have sufficient income."

Sybille wrote the hardship letter, a really good sob story, especially since it was all true. Clarence put together a comp sheet showing what the lender could expect to net from a short sale compared to a foreclosure. As is usually the case, the short sale made much more sense.

He included Sybille's bank statements, pay stubs, and 1040 IRS forms. He attached BPOs (broker price opinions) of the property (although the lender would surely want its own). He also included a HUD-1 statement (Housing and Urban Development closing form required on all residential real estate sales), which broke down the closing costs and showed a 5 percent commission to him on each one plus escrow and other fees.

Then he contacted the lender's loss mitigation committee. Lenders were having so many losses that all the big ones had created committees to handle short sales. The loss mitigation committees had separate phone numbers and assigned negotiators to handle the load. He quickly faxed in the package.

He had an answer two days later. (It was December 2008, and by then many lenders had their acts together and were processing short sales in days.) It was a tentative approval subject to a BPO. That happened within the week, and the lender was ready to go. Sybille came in and signed the papers releasing her property. She was out from under!

In her case the only ding to her credit was that she missed a few payments. The lender hadn't even filed a *notice of default*, which admittedly is rare in short sale cases. There was also no demand that she pay back any of the money in the form of a deficiency agreement. However, her accountant warned her that she might owe a tax liability on the amount the lender had forgiven.

Of course, she lost her original $100,000 investment plus roughly another $50,000 in the course of trying to keep up the payments.

MORAL

What goes up fast, usually comes down fast, and that includes real estate prices. Mortgages that offer high leverage and unreasonably low payments always come with great risk. And if the market turns, the most optimistic plans can quickly come unraveled.

Perhaps you see yourself mirrored in one of these stories. Or perhaps your tale is quite different. In the course of writing this book I came across dozens of different scenarios, all of which required short sales to solve them. In the following chapters we'll see just how to accomplish a short sale and how it might save you a lot of stress, heartaches, and years of bad credit.

Seven Steps to a Short Sale

There are seven steps you should follow to complete a short sale. These are:

1. Use a preliminary net sheet (PNS) to see if you really are under water. (See Chapter 3.)
2. Find a good real estate agent who specializes in short sales (see Chapter 4), or sell the property yourself.
3. Prepare your property to be sold, and prepare yourself to move. (See Chapter 5.)
4. Find a buyer for your home at market price. (See Chapter 10.)
5. Write and sign an authorization letter so your agent and others can contact and deal with your lender. (See Chapter 6.)
6. Have your agent (or do it yourself) prepare a short sale package to be sent to your lender which includes documentation of your financial condition as well as a hardship letter. (See Chapter 7.)
7. Sign the papers and get out from under!

Sometimes sellers have more than one mortgage on a property—a second, and perhaps a third, and a fourth, and so on. There also may be taxes and other liens on the property. To find out how these can be handled, see Chapter 2.

How a Short Sale Can Help You

A successful short sale can be a blessing. If you don't believe it, consider the alternative.

The usual alternative to a short sale is foreclosure. That's a really mean beast of a thing to happen to anyone. And it's nothing you want to have happen to you.

What's so wrong with foreclosure?

Think of elephants. The old adage is that an elephant never forgets—it has a terrific memory. Injure an elephant in its youth, and, according to those who should know, it will remember you with animosity its entire life. Lenders are something like that when it comes to foreclosures.

When you lose a property to foreclosure, it is recorded as a major problem on your credit report. It stands out as something that's just as bad and perhaps even worse than a bankruptcy. Not only will other creditors see it there, but every mortgage lender whom you might go to for a new loan will see it as well. Mortgage lenders *always* get reports from the three major credit reporting agencies (Experian, TransUnion, and Equifax), which invariably pull up records of a foreclosure. In other words, your foreclosure gets remembered. There isn't a lender around who won't learn of it.

How long does a foreclosure remain on your credit report? According to most credit reporting companies with whom I've checked, it's 7 to 10 years. However, my experience with people who've had foreclosures is that the period of time can be almost indefinite. Sometimes you get a credit report 15 years later and up pops that foreclosure report. And once it appears and the lender sees it, even if it happened a long time ago, getting that lender to overlook it will be nearly impossible.

Consider it from the perspective of a new lender.

If once you allowed your home to go through foreclosure, no matter how long ago, what are the chances that if times get tough, you'll let the house go again? Lenders say that it just gets easier and easier.

What it all comes down to is, why should a lender take a chance with you a second time? That's where the lenders' long memories come in. Once a lender is injured by a foreclosure, other lenders never seem to forget.

Remember, no matter how ridiculous it may seem to you and me, lenders always feel that, regardless of circumstances, you should keep making the payments. It doesn't matter if you get sick, if the market turns you upside down, if you lose your job, or if some other dire thing happens. From the lenders' perspective, all they really care about are performing loans, the ones where the monthly payment comes in regularly for the full amount on time. Don't make a payment and it's like your loan caught a cold. Go through foreclosure and it's like your loan got cancer.

Once you have hurt them in the past by not making payments (and *forcing* them to foreclose), many lenders just don't want to give you another chance, another mortgage.

All of which is to say if you ever hope to buy another home and don't have the resources to pay cash for it (a situation that happens to just about all of us), you'll need to get a new mortgage from a lender. And that lender, when it sees that you had a foreclosure, may very well say no, even if by then you've reestablished otherwise exemplary credit.

TIP

In the past new lenders would allow you to submit a letter of explanation (excuses, really) regarding a foreclosure—you lost your job, the house burned down, the mortgage reset and you couldn't make the payments. (Scratch that last one—lenders are unlikely to be sympathetic to it.) However, in recent years lenders have tended to refuse even to consider letters of explanation. In other words, you probably won't be able to talk your way out of an old foreclosure.

As I say above, mortgage lenders are like elephants. Allow your home to go into foreclosure and chances are they'll remember that for a very long time and may refuse to deal with you because of it.

Of course, it's not quite so bad with other lenders such as those who offer credit cards and auto loans. According to some I checked with, the magic number is just two to three years. Show stable credit for only two years after a foreclosure, and you may get a new credit card, maybe even a new car loan.

The trouble, of course, is showing stable credit when you can't get any credit.

A Successful Short Sale Story

Jay had a house in Southern California that he and his wife bought in 2005. They paid $650,000 for it. By 2008 it was worth only $440,000.

That wasn't the big problem, however. They loved the house and could have stayed there for years. It was perfect for their family. (They had three children.)

The real problem was that Jay's wife, who had a good job in a wholesale distributorship, lost her job. And at about the same time Jay's company began laying off workers and cut back on his overtime.

Suddenly they couldn't afford the house they were living in. And they couldn't sell it or refinance because they were under water. (They had not only a first mortgage but a home equity loan in the form of a second mortgage as well.) But they kept making their payments. (Toward the end they were late a few times, but they never failed to make a payment.)

So, they contacted an expert short sale agent who advertised on the Internet. He came to their house and explained the whole short sale process. Then he listed their property at a good price.

He produced a buyer within a month. Then the agent put together a strong package and submitted it to their *second* mortgage lender. In it he detailed a payoff that included $500 to the second mortgage holder as an incentive to sign off. (See "How to Get Holders of Junior Mortgages..." for more on this.) The package also included a hardship letter in which Jay explained how difficult it was to lose their house, but with his wife's lost job and his fewer overtime hours, they simply could not afford it. They had no choice but do a short sale. (Just to be safe, Jay got an attorney to review the deal.) Once the second mortgage lender had agreed to release its interest, the agent submitted the offer to the lender of the first mortgage—the big mortgage on the property.

They got an affirmative answer from the lender within two weeks.

Then it was a matter of waiting for escrow to close, finding a good rental and moving, and closing the deal.

By the time the deal closed, they were in the process of not making their next house payment and would have been behind a month. As it was, they fell behind only a couple of times.

After the sale, Jay was a little bitter about having lost the family's home. And he pointed out that their credit score had taken a hundred-point hit. But for him, credit was really important and not having a foreclosure and the huge long-term hit it would given him was all important.

"We can always bring back our credit after being late a few times on our payments. But, that's nothing compared to what would have happened if we had a foreclosure on our record."

MORAL

Short sales can work out, even when you've never missed a payment. A lot depends on your taking quick, appropriate action.

What About Just Walking Away?

Having elaborated on the perils of foreclosure, I'm sure that a certain number of readers are still wondering, "Is all the hassle of a short sale worthwhile?"

After all, if you are under water on a house (owe more than it's worth), maybe it's better to simply walk away—just move out and let the lender take it back. After all, that would stop the lender from hassling you. And it could go a long way toward restoring your peace of mind.

I'm certainly not going to say that walking is a good idea. It forces the lender to foreclose, and I've just explained why a foreclosure is a bad idea. On the other hand, I've never heard anyone say that walking away is illegal. And some clever sellers who are willing to accept the consequences have pulled it off with panache. For example, as we've seen, one of the biggest consequences of just walking away is the inability to buy another house because you can't get financing. So these sellers have bought another house while their credit was still good, *before* they began missing payments on their first house.

Typically this has occurred when the market has collapsed. They might be able to buy the home down the street or even next door for two-thirds or even half of what they owe on their present home. Then they simply switch homes and stop making payments on their old home.

Yes, they lose it to foreclosure. Yes, they probably won't be able to finance another home for from 7 to 10 years. Yes, their credit is likely ruined.

But they already have their next home—they just bought it. And if they're prepared to stay there for 7 to 10 years, then what's the problem?

Furthermore, if they kept making payments on a couple of credit cards, chances are those credit card companies, while perhaps reducing their credit limits and increasing the interest rate, will keep honoring the cards. So they've got some credit. And, finally, they've gotten out from under an overwhelming burden of high payments and a loan that's more than their old house is worth. Why not do it?

I see the reasoning and understand the motivation, but I also know there's a better way. Why not simply move forward with a short sale on the old house? The short sale will avoid the problems of a foreclosure and ruined credit. It, too, will get you out from under, but without walking away.

Yes, walking away is quick. But it's also dirty. If things go wrong in the future—such as job layoff, illness, or even divorce—and you need your good credit, you could really be up the creek without a paddle.

Because of the alternatives, I have to say that walking away is to be avoided.

How Short Sales Are Done

When you obtain a mortgage or, as is more commonly used in most of the country, a trust deed (we have more to say about mortgages vs. trust deeds shortly), you *hypothecate* your property. That essentially means that you put the property up as collateral to a lender while not losing your rights to occupy it or rent it out to someone else. What you essentially say is, "Mr. Lender, in exchange for you giving me the money to buy (or refinance) my home, I'll give you the right to take ownership of it *if* I don't make the payments and meet the other terms of our contract." Don't make the payments and the lender forecloses and takes your homes. It's not exactly like making a deal with the devil, but it's not entirely unlike it, either.

In a successful short sale, on the other hand, your home is sold to an outside buyer, and the mortgage(s) is paid off with any shortage often forgiven. You no longer own it; the foreclosing loan is gone, and, hence, there is no foreclosure to go on your record.

The process, however, can be tricky, and there are several things you need to know. One of the most important is the order of mortgages.

The Order of Mortgages

You've probably heard of a first mortgage and a second mortgage and a third and so on. But what exactly does that mean? And how does it affect foreclosure and short sales?

The order of mortgages is really simple to understand. It's the order in which they were recorded on the property at the county recorder's office. The first mortgage to be recorded in time is called a first. The next mortgage to be recorded in time is called a second. If there's yet another one recorded, it becomes a third, and so on.

The order in which the mortgages are recorded is a critical factor when it comes to foreclosure. In foreclosure the property is auctioned off to the highest bidder. The money that's realized from the sale is distributed in the following order:

The first mortgage has first claim. If there's not enough to
pay off the first, then all the other mortgages go without—
they get no money at all!

If there's more than enough to pay the first, then any money
left over goes to pay the second. If there's not enough to
fully pay off the second, then the third and any other junior mortgages go entirely without.

If there's more than enough to pay the first and the second,
then the third gets some of it. And so on

Note, it's not a democracy. The various mortgages do not split
up the proceeds from the sale. Rather, it all depends on which
mortgage was recorded earliest when it comes time to divvy up
the money.

TIP

The amount paid off also doesn't depend on the size of the mortgage. While
usually a first is the biggest mortgage, it doesn't necessarily have to be that way.
The first could just be, for example, $10,000, and the second $100,000. In this
case, the first still gets paid off first in foreclosure.

The reason this is important is that many properties have more
than one mortgage. (Indeed some have four, five, and more mortgages!) Each one has to be in some way satisfied in order to have a
successful short sale.

Short Sale with Three Mortgages

Jon bought a home with a nothing-down mortgage. The house
quickly went up in price, so he got a HELOC (home equity line of
credit), which was recorded as a second mortgage. (Remember the
order of mortgages?)

Then Jon wanted a new car, and since he had maxed out the
HELOC, he got a third mortgage to pay for it. All went well until
the real estate market collapsed and his home dropped in value.

First	$300,000		
Second	50,000		
Third	20,000		
Total	$370,000	vs. current value	$260,000

Figure 2.1 Mortgage vs. value on Jon's home

The home lost 30 percent of its value. The mortgage structure is shown in Figure 2.1.

Then Jon lost his job and found that he couldn't make his mortgage payments. So he stopped making payments on all three mortgages.

In a normal market scenario where the borrower has sufficient equity in the property and stops making payments, the holder of the most junior mortgage (the third in this case) will foreclose first. The reason is that if the second forecloses, it will only seek to get enough money to pay itself, even if there was extra equity left. That could wipe out the third. If the first forecloses, it could wipe out the second and third. Therefore, to protect itself, the most junior mortgage, in this case the third, forecloses on the home.

TIP The junior mortgage that forecloses typically begins making payments on the senior mortgage(s), thereby keeping the holders of the mortgages from foreclosing. It then adds those payments to its payoff.

However, in Jon's case, he has no equity in the house. Because of the depressed price, in an auction sale no one would bid on the second or the third mortgage. The junior mortgages' interest in the house has been effectively wiped out by the price drop. So, since they have no incentive to foreclose, they simply give up and don't. Rather, the first, which would still receive money in a foreclosure sale, forecloses. That's why we primarily speak of dealing with the first in a short sale.

To get on with our story, Jon eventually finds a buyer and gets an agreement with the lender of the first mortgage to accept a short payoff, as we've seen in previous examples.

But what about the holders of the second and third mortgages?

Remember, in a foreclosure auction they would be wiped out. But here we're not talking about a foreclosure auction; we're talking about a short sale. Here when the lender of the first accepts a short payoff to release its interest, the holders of the second and third remain. Indeed, they actually advance in order. Once the original first is released, the second becomes the new first, the third the new second, and so on.

Problems in a Short Sale

In a mishandled short sale, there might be a release on the first mortgage only to have it discovered that the second and the third were still in place, which could and would immediately begin foreclosure proceedings (because suddenly they would have equity interest in the property). No buyer would accept this.

Be sure you understand what's happening here. Because there is no foreclosure, the second and third mortgages remain of record and do not get removed. The original first, however, does get removed when it releases Jon after the payoff. With the first gone, the other mortgages move up and have a viable interest in the home.

It would be like jumping out of the frying pan into the fire. You can be sure the holders of the junior mortgages would be eager and ready to pounce on Jon (and the new owner) to get some money out of the property, which would now be worth far more than their combined debt ($70,000 in this case).

Therefore to make the deal safely, Jon needs to get releases not only on the first mortgage but also on all junior mortgages (and all other liens).

get full releases on all mortgages and other liens on your property
conclude a short sale.

Since any savvy new buyer is likely to insist on clear title, which could only occur
when all the old liens and mortgages are released, it's unlikely that the first
would get paid off without the other mortgages and liens getting taken care of.

How to Get Holders of Junior Mortgages (and Other Lien Holders) to Release

There are really only three ways to get holders of junior mortgages and other lien holders to release:

1. **Ask nicely.**

   After all, the interest of the junior mortgage holders and
   other lien holders has presumably been wiped out by the
   drop in the property value. They aren't going to foreclose,
   because they'll get nothing out of it. You know that, and
   they know you know. Everyone also knows you're getting
   nothing out of the deal. So the decent thing for them to
   do is to sign a release. When presented with the facts in a
   nice way, some junior mortgage and other lien holders
   will do just that.

2. **Offer a cash payment.**

   Remember, they don't have to sign. They can simply hold
   out and let your home go to foreclosure. After all, they get
   nothing either way. So if they refuse to sign a release, offer
   them some cash, perhaps $500 or $1,000. That's more
   than they would get otherwise and may be enough of an
   incentive to get them to sign a release.

   Where do you get the cash?

Sometimes the foreclosing lender will pay the other lien holders off. Some institutional first mortgage holders will offer an allowance in a short sale to pay off junior mortgage holders and other lien holders. It might be $1,000, $500, or more or less. Once you strike an arrangement with the junior lien holders, you write it into your package and present it to the foreclosing lender. You can only try.

If the foreclosing lender won't budge, then the only other source of cash is you.

3. **Offer a promissory note.**

The foreclosing lender won't offer any cash, you don't have any, so your last best hope is a promissory note. You might offer to pay off the junior mortgage holder(s) $1,000 over 10 years at 3 percent interest. (That's only $9.66 a month). Is that worthwhile enough to you get a release? Perhaps it is. And the junior mortgage and other lien holders might just go for it. After all, it beats nothing.

TIP

Although agents often negotiate for you with a lender in this fashion, it probably should be done under the purview of an attorney. This is a good time to get an attorney to advise you. (Sometimes one will work for you under the assumption that the lender of the first mortgage will pay his or her fees when a short sale is concluded.)

Deficiency Judgment

There's yet another trap in a short sale, and that's a deficiency judgment, or at least the threat of it. Here, in some cases when the foreclosing lender doesn't net enough to pay off the full loan amount, as part of its court action, it can get a judgment against you for the unpaid balance. Thus, for example, if the payoff to the lender is

$100,000 short, in theory the lender might be able to get a judgment against you for that amount and with it could tie up your other property or even garnish your wages, after the foreclosure.

TIP

Many states have purchase money mortgage rules. These specify that if the mortgage being foreclosed on was used to purchase a home, no deficiency judgment is allowed. California is such a state. Other states, such as Arizona, outright ban deficiency judgments. See the resources at the end of Chapter 11 to see where your state falls. (In California when the lender uses the more common non-judicial foreclosure process, no deficiency judgment can be obtained against you—see Chapter 11.)

Of course, the vast majority of homeowners seeking short sales do not have just one issue, the house payment. Rather, their stories tend to be catastrophic across the board. Not only can't they make the mortgage payment, but they tend to be behind on medical bills, car payments, credit card debt, and so on. In other words, missing the mortgage payment was symptomatic of a general credit crisis in their lives, not just an isolated incident. See Figure 2.2 for information on foreclosures nationwide.

Defaulters were not always people who had lost their jobs or had gotten sick and thus lost their source of income, although many were in that situation. Often they had gotten themselves into tremendous debt by borrowing to maintain a lifestyle that they simply could not afford. Easy credit during the period prior to the crash of the U.S. economy made it possible. And tightening of credit after the crash exacerbated the situation. As noted, many people who were facing foreclosure were also having to deal with collection agencies coming after them for not making payments on their credit cards, auto loans, and other debts.

Foreclosing lenders know this; hence, often they simply will not even bother with a deficiency judgment. They just will not pursue it.

Rate rank	State name	Total foreclosure filings	Total properties with filings	% Change from 2007	% Change from 2006	% Housing units (foreclosure rate)
—	U.S.	3,157,806	2,330,483	81.24	224.80	1.84
43	Alabama	8,436	7,764	39.34	184.19	0.37
31	Alaska	2,265	1,946	46.10	96.76	0.70
3	Arizona	152,621	116,911	203.13	655.04	4.49
23	Arkansas	16,611	14,277	122.87	198.06	1.12
4	California	837,665	523,624	109.86	497.91	3.97
5	Colorado	66,795	50,396	27.90	61.41	2.41
15	Connecticut	25,510	21,925	84.87	570.49	1.53
33	Delaware	2,998	2,516	151.85*	701.27*	0.66
	District of Columbia	4,631	4,182	438.22*	3245.60*	1.48
2	Florida	501,396	385,309	133.11	411.68	4.52
8	Georgia	116,225	85,254	44.36	117.07	2.20
34	Hawaii	3,346	3,185	229.71	489.81	0.64
19	Idaho	11,272	8,512	133.85	302.08	1.38
9	Illinois	115,063	99,488	54.70	126.01	1.91
11	Indiana	61,141	45,937	64.18	113.59	1.67
40	Iowa	6,405	5,385	31.25	135.77	0.41
36	Kansas	7,983	6,218	155.46	179.96	0.51
42	Kentucky	8,820	7,244	41.90	45.46	0.38
41	Louisiana	7,837	7,129	79.66	111.42	0.39
38	Maine	3,171	2,851	896.85*	5602.00*	0.41
18	Maryland	41,582	32,338	71.29	945.18	1.41
14	Massachusetts	53,797	44,342	150.00	577.08	1.64
6	Michigan	145,365	106,058	21.61	107.89	2.35
26	Minnesota	23,716	20,282	75.50	336.74	0.89
46	Mississippi	2,364	2,293	62.74	181.35	0.18
20	Missouri	42,054	31,254	33.04	139.11	1.19

(continued on next page)

Figure 2.2 U.S. Foreclosure Market Data by State—2008
Data source: RealtyTrac, Inc.

Rate rank	State name	Total foreclosure filings	Total properties with filings	% Change from 2007	% Change from 2006	% Housing units (foreclosure rate)
44	Montana	1,220	1,246	8.35	32.55	0.29
39	Nebraska	3,326	3,190	−12.27	25.84	0.41
1	Nevada	123,989	77,693	125.74	529.50	7.29
22	New Hampshire	8,018	6,636	436.03*	5430.00*	1.13
10	New Jersey	69,612	62,514	101.20	186.84	1.80
37	New Mexico	4,543	3,727	24.48	38.29	0.44
35	New York	55,641	50,032	29.32	129.23	0.63
27	North Carolina	41,750	33,819	16.21	153.14	0.84
47	North Dakota	391	371	48.40	148.99	0.12
7	Ohio	146,099	113,570	26.22	155.40	2.25
29	Oklahoma	16,059	12,465	50.98	32.86	0.78
21	Oregon	25,049	18,001	112.75	168.67	1.13
32	Pennsylvania	42,949	37,210	127.18	68.88	0.68
17	Rhode Island	7,334	6,583	258.16*	1525.43*	1.46
30	South Carolina	16,136	14,995	253.07*	220.41*	0.76
48	South Dakota	405	402	1575.00*	793.33*	0.11
12	Tennessee	51,496	44,153	70.38	127.87	1.65
24	Texas	129,201	96,157	13.84	14.96	1.04
13	Utah	18,657	14,836	99.46	68.25	1.65
50	Vermont	124	137	372.41*	705.88*	0.04
16	Virginia	67,695	49,011	200.55	1746.68*	1.52
25	Washington	32,271	26,058	71.61	116.64	0.97
49	West Virginia	687	685	48.91	170.75	0.08
28	Wisconsin	25,164	19,695	62.33	249.02	0.78
45	Wyoming	921	677	90.17	165.49	0.28

Actual increase may not be as high due to data collection changes or improvements.

Figure 2.2 U.S. Foreclosure Market Data by State—2008
Data source: RealtyTrac, Inc.

On the other hand, a nasty lender can use the threat of a deficiency judgment to get something more out of you in a short sale. For example, the lender may point out that if it forecloses judicially (through court action), it may be able to get the deficiency judgment. If there's a short sale, it can't. Therefore, as an incentive to grant the short sale, it wants you to sign a promissory note (since it knows you undoubtedly have no cash) to pay it a set amount, say $5,000 with interest over the next 10 years. Sign the note, and it'll move forward with the short sale. Don't sign, and it won't, and it will hold the threat of a deficiency judgment after foreclosure over you.

What do you do?

Negotiate with the lender. You can do it yourself. Or a good attorney (or sometimes an agent) may be able to get the lender to see the light. If that fails, determine whether signing the promissory note is worth the short sale to you. It might or might not be.

TRAP

Some foreclosing lenders (usually the first mortgage) will not even consider a short sale until all of the other mortgage and lien holders have agreed to give releases. Thus, when there's more than one mortgage on the property, often the place to start is with the junior ones.

The Short Sale as a Solution

As this book contends, one solution to stopping foreclosure and salvaging your credit is a short sale—the mortgage is paid off, and you're out from under. The trick, of course, is to get the lender to accept that short payoff.

Does the lender want to help you do that?

Very often the answer, unfortunately, is no. The lender has other priorities, and it's helpful to understand them. The lender's motivation to accept a short sale:

- Is *not* to save your credit.
- Is *not* to save you money.
- Is *not* to help you out.
- *Is* to save the lender money and time.

Thus in order to get the lender to agree to a short sale, it's better to show why it's to the lender's advantage than why it's to your advantage.

Will a Short Sale Work for You?

The majority of sellers who need a short sale are already in foreclosure—most, but not all. If, for example, your mortgage resets to a much higher payment or you lose your ability to make your old payment (job loss, divorce, illness, and so on), you might not yet be in foreclosure. But you can see it coming down the road.

In that case, you'd probably be wise to sell or refinance your property. Of course, if you're under water or close to it, selling or refinancing becomes impossible (because you owe more than your home is worth). And, hence, a short sale pops up as a solution to your problem. (There are other alternatives; see Chapter 12.) If that is your situation, rest assured that you are not alone. As many as 10 percent of all properties in the United States were in or nearing foreclosure by 2009 (detailed in Figure 3.1).

Rate rank	State	Metro name	Total properties with filings	% Housing units (foreclosure rate)	% Change from 2007
1	CA	Stockton	21,127	9.46	99.16
2	NV	Las Vegas/Paradise	67,223	8.89	121.31
3	CA	Riverside/San Bernardino	112,284	8.02	117.02
4	CA	Bakersfield	16,208	6.17	115.42
5	AZ	Phoenix/Mesa	97,684	6.02	220.77
6	FL	Fort Lauderdale	47,387	5.95	127.81
7	FL	Orlando	46,843	5.48	195.84
8	FL	Miami	49,697	5.21	96.46
9	CA	Sacramento	39,876	5.20	67.74
10	MI	Detroit/Livonia/Dearborn	38,106	4.52	−7.67
11	FL	Sarasota/Bradenton/Venice	17,256	4.50	153.58
12	CA	Fresno	12,571	4.20	102.50
13	FL	Tampa/St Petersburg/Clearwater	53,630	4.14	122.66
14	CA	Oakland	38,797	4.09	99.34
15	CA	San Diego	44,931	3.99	122.24
16	FL	Palm Beach	23,399	3.71	96.33
17	GA	Atlanta/Sandy Springs/Marietta	67,007	3.26	33.29
18	TN-MS-AR	Memphis	17,245	3.21	52.73
19	CO	Denver/Aurora	32,920	3.20	23.61
20	CA	Ventura	8,422	3.11	94.01
21	CA	Orange	31,300	3.06	150.38
22	FL	Jacksonville	17,025	2.99	78.46
23	DC-MD-VA-WV	Washington/Arlington/Alexandria	50,148	2.97	160.79*
24	OH	Cleveland/Lorain/Elyria/Mentor	27,693	2.94	−0.56
25	MI	Warren/Farmington Hills/Troy	30,817	2.92	42.63
26	CA	Los Angeles/Long Beach	96,974	2.89	113.53
27	IN	Indianapolis	20,316	2.76	39.24
28	OH	Akron	8,259	2.69	16.60
29	OH	Toledo	7,957	2.67	38.24
30	OH	Columbus	19,489	2.54	40.99
31	IL	Lake/Kenosha	6,323	2.52	70.06
32	CA	San Jose/Sunnyvale/Santa Clara	15,633	2.49	153.25
33	IL	Chicago	77,226	2.49	53.38
34	OH	Dayton	9,231	2.43	18.16
35	NJ	Newark	19,607	2.33	123.57

Figure 3.1 Top 100 U.S. Metro Foreclosure Market Data–2008
Data source: RealtyTrac, Inc.

Rate rank	State	Metro name	Total properties with filings	% Housing units (foreclosure rate)	% Change from 2007
36	MA	Essex	6,538	2.21	190.45
37	AZ	Tucson	9,043	2.16	113.33
38	WA	Tacoma	6,669	2.16	114.64
39	IN	Gary	6,032	2.12	93.71
40	MA	Worcester	6,344	2.02	105.04
41	NJ	Camden	9,026	1.87	164.30
42	OH-KY-IN	Cincinnati	16,731	1.85	27.53
43	CT	Newhaven/Milford	6,314	1.81	66.60
44	MA	Boston/Quincy	13,332	1.77	161.10
45	MO-IL	St Louis	21,645	1.77	40.15
46	UT	Salt Lake City	6,628	1.72	79.52
47	CT	Bridgeport/Stamford/Norwalk	5,874	1.68	140.84
48	WI	Milwaukee/Waukesha/West Allis	10,181	1.57	55.94
49	MO-KS	Kansas City	13,609	1.56	35.06
50	MA	Springfield	4,331	1.54	118.19
51	TX	Houston/Baytown/Sugarland	31,981	1.52	28.35
52	TN	Nashville/Davidson	9,434	1.51	77.97
53	TX	Fort Worth/Arlington	11,540	1.50	−6.14
54	AR	Little Rock/North Little Rock	4,336	1.49	60.47
55	TX	Dallas	22,992	1.49	−7.74
56	RI	Providence/New Bedford	6,583	1.46	257.97
57	NC-SC	Charlotte/Gastonia	9,802	1.45	3.99
58	NJ	Edison	13,399	1.44	73.49
59	MN-WI	Minneapolis/St Paul/Bloomington	18,450	1.41	70.86
60	MD	Bethesda/Frederick/Gaithersburg	6,098	1.37	103.33
61	CT	Hartford	6,305	1.29	70.45
62	NC	Greensboro/Highpoint	3,935	1.29	27.84
63	MA	Cambridge/Newton/Framingham	7,585	1.28	161.01
64	SC	Charleston	3,501	1.28	317.28*
65	OR-WA	Portland/Vancouver/Beaverton	10,684	1.22	106.97
66	OK	Tulsa	4,777	1.22	35.25
67	SC	Greenville	3,100	1.17	1355.40*
68	TN	Knoxville	3,542	1.17	95.37
69	NY	Poughkeepsie/Newburgh/Middletown	2,826	1.16	330.79*

(continued on next page)

Figure 3.1 Top 100 U.S. Metro Foreclosure Market Data–2008 *(cont.)*

Rate rank	State	Metro name	Total properties with filings	% Housing units (foreclosure rate)	% Change from 2007
70	TX	San Antonio	8,033	1.09	4.90
71	NC	Raleigh/Cary	4,444	1.09	14.42
72	MD	Baltimore/Towson	11,776	1.07	47.14
73	VA	Richmond	5,159	1.03	468.17*
74	NY	Suffolk/Nassau	9,984	1.00	2.93
75	CA	San Francisco	7,168	0.98	105.68
76	LA	New Orleans	4,382	0.98	89.04
77	PA	Philadelphia	15,659	0.97	98.24
78	OK	Oklahoma City	4,977	0.97	22.77
79	VA-NC	Norfolk/Virginia Beach/ Newport News	5,662	0.95	207.55*
80	TX	Austin/Round Rock	5,737	0.94	11.05
81	PA	Pittsburgh	10,013	0.91	147.85
82	SC	Columbia	2,704	0.89	181.37*
83	NY	Rochester	3,825	0.87	12.37
84	WA	Seattle/Bellevue/Everett	9,239	0.86	84.19
85	DE-MD-NJ	Wilmington	2,347	0.84	131.92
86	TX	McAllen/Edinburg/Pharr	1,982	0.83	549.84*
87	KY-IN	Louisville	4,285	0.79	34.03
88	NM	Albuquerque	2,688	0.77	21.24
89	NE-IA	Omaha/Council Bluffs	2,613	0.76	−13.51
90	NY	Buffalo/Cheektowaga/Tonawanda	3,842	0.74	73.85*
91	NY-NJ	New York/Wayne/White Plains	31,165	0.71	38.09
92	KS	Wichita	1,698	0.67	156.50
93	NY	Albany/Schenectady/Troy	2,416	0.64	151.67
94	PA	Scranton/Wilkes-Barre/Hazleton	1,620	0.63	136.50
95	TX	El Paso	1,408	0.56	12.01
96	PA	Allentown/Bethlehem/Easton	1,553	0.50	195.25
97	HI	Honolulu	1,647	0.50	218.57
98	AL	Birmingham/Hoover	2,163	0.47	−8.00
99	NY	Syracuse	1,028	0.36	182.42
100	LA	Baton Rouge	1,107	0.35	34.51

*Actual increase may not be as high due to data collection changes or improvements

Figure 3.1 Top 100 U.S. Metro Foreclosure Market Data–2008 *(cont.)*

In this chapter we look at your own situation to see if a short sale is going to help. The best way to find out is to create a PNS (preliminary net sheet). Any real estate agent should be able to do it for you when you consider listing your property. However, you can easily do it yourself without having to disclose your finances to anyone.

The purpose of the PNS is to show you how much you will net from your home when you sell. Unfortunately, the bottom line of this sheet in this economy and real state market too often ends up negative. The good news is that it fairly accurately tells you how far under water you are and how big a short payoff you're going to have to ask for from the lender.

Until you know the results of the preliminary net sheet, you won't truly know if need a short sale or not. It might just turn out that you actually have some equity left in your home. If that's the case, you can pursue a conventional sale or you may be able to refinance.

Another advantage of the PNS is that it gathers together all the information you're going to need to proceed with a short sale once you decided it's the best alternative.

Let's take a look at how you score on the preliminary net sheet. See Figure 3.2.

If the last figure is positive, congratulations! It means that you still have equity left in your home and that you can probably sell it in the conventional manner or possibly refinance.

If, however, the last figure is a negative (and in today's market it often is), you're under water. You owe more in a sale than you can recoup. You are looking at a short sale to get out from under.

How Do I Handle Expenses in a Short Sale?

Regardless of whether you have a conventional sale or a short sale, there are going to be expenses, and they are always pretty much the same. You're going to need to find a buyer for your house (or

Your name: _____

Home address: _____

Your phone number: _____

Anticipated sale price: $ _____

As determined by comparison with other properties sold. [See Chapter 7.]

Existing financing

First mortgage lender: _____

    Phone number: _____

    Address: _____

    Account number: _____

    Initial contact (if you know): _____

    Amount still owed plus back payments and penalties: $ _____

Second mortgage lender: _____

    Phone number: _____

    Address: _____

    Account number: _____

    Initial contact (if you know): _____

    Amount still owed plus back payments and penalties: $ _____

    Payoff willing to accept: $ _____

Third mortgage lender: _____

    Phone number: _____

    Address: _____

    Account number: _____

    Initial contact (if you know): _____

    Amount still owed plus back payments and penalties: $ _____

    Payoff willing to accept: $ _____

Fourth mortgage lender: _____

    Address: _____

    Account number: _____

    Initial contact (if you know): _____

    Amount still owed plus back payments and penalties: $ _____

    Payoff willing to accept: $ _____

Figure 3.2 Preliminary net sheet

Other debt (secured by the property)

Lien holder name:_____

    Phone number: _____

    Address: _____

    Account number:_____

    Initial contact (if you know): _____

    Amount still owed: $ _____

    Payoff willing to accept: $ _____

Lien holder name:_____

    Phone number: _____

    Address: _____

    Account number: _____

    Initial contact (if you know): _____

    Amount still owed: $ _____

    Payoff willing to accept: $ _____

Other amounts owed

Back taxes: $ _____

Back home owner's fees: $ _____

PMI (Private Mortgage Insurance) fees: $ _____

Other: $ _____

Costs of sale

Real estate commission: $ _____

                                                 (At 5 or 6 percent)

Escrow charges: $ _____

Title insurance: $ _____

Document recording: $ _____

Other fees (if known): $ _____

Total expenses of selling $ _____

                                                 (Add all the charges)

Subtract expenses from value of property $ _____

Figure 3.2 Preliminary net sheet *(cont.)*

have an agent find a buyer). And in order to facilitate the sale, there will need to be an escrow, which typically costs a few thousand dollars. You'll have to guarantee clear title to the property, which is usually in the form of title insurance, which again will probably cost a few thousand dollars. In Chapter 2 we discuss payoffs to other mortgage and lien holders. And there are also other closing costs from recording fees to document preparation.

TRAP

Who pays for title insurance and escrow—the buyer or the seller—is normally a matter of tradition determined by the area of the country you're in. Today, however, very often both expenses are split.

All these costs are in addition to back taxes and other fees that you may have incurred.

Many sellers when they see all the costs detailed on the PNS simply shake their head in wonder. If all their equity has been erased by a drop in the market value of real estate, how are those fees going to be paid? Who is going to pay them?

One thing is certain, there isn't a seller in a thousand who is willing or able to take additional money out of pocket to pay them on a short sale. After all, you're getting nothing out of the sale, save for your good credit. *You* are certainly not going to pay them!

The Money Comes from the New Buyer and His or Her New Mortgage, but Ultimately from the Foreclosing Lender

The only party remaining who can pay the closing costs on your home is the buyer. However, the buyer has set a price, and everything has to come out of that price. Hence, for every new expense that comes out of that price, the net to the lender goes down. The more expenses and the pricier they are, the less the lender gets.

Thus, for practical purposes, it's the foreclosing lender who determines what gets paid. It all comes down to what that lender will allow. For example, it's up to the lender of the foreclosing mortgage to decide whether to allow for the closing costs and how much.

If you're wondering who pays the sales commission, again, it's certainly not going to be you. As noted, you're getting nothing out of the deal save your credit score. You're certainly not going to pull money out of your wallet to pay an agent.

Yet, it usually takes an agent to sell the property. And agents won't work for free. Hence, once again, the only party who can allow payment to the agent is the lender of the foreclosing mortgage. In almost all short sales involving an agent, one of the expenses the lender must approve is the sales commission. (Interestingly, many lenders will approve only a maximum of 5 percent commission, not the 6 percent commission that many agents seek to charge.)

How the Lender Sees It

For a moment, let's look at a different kind of net sheet, the kind that the lender prepares for itself. It's quite a bit different from the one that you'll use to see if you're under water. See Figure 3.3.

Notice that the way the lender figures it is slightly different. The lender begins with the outstanding loan balance and then subtracts the short sale price and all the other expenses of closing the deal. This results in its net and its loss.

From the lender's perspective, you don't pay the commission; it's the lender's expense. You don't pay back taxes and insurance; the lender does. You don't pay the other closing costs; the lender does.

Of course, the lender is most interested in keeping down costs. Hence, regardless of what you put into your own net sheet, the

Mortgage balance outstanding	$400,000	
Short sale price	$300,000	
Less Estimated Expenses To Close		
Interest lost	15,000	
Closing costs	8,000	
RE (Real Estate) broker fees	30,000	
Maintenance	5,000	
Utilities	3,000	
Property taxes	2,500	
Insurance	500	
Payment to lien holders	10,000	
Net to lender	226,000	−226,000
Lender's loss on short sale		174,000

Figure 3.3 Lender's net sheet on short sale

lender is likely to change it for its net sheet. For example, while you may negotiate a commission rate with the agent, it's up to the lender to allow it. The lender could easily say that paying a real estate agent 6 percent is too high. It's only willing to allow a payment of 5 percent. Now it's up to the agent to either accept less or scuttle the deal. In my experience, almost always the agent will accept less.

In short, it's up to the lender to determine what it will allow in terms of closing expenses in order to make the deal. Ultimately, for it to go forward, the lender must feel that taking a loss, in this case $174,000, is more worthwhile than letting the property go through foreclosure, where it could lose even more. (See Chapter 7.) If the lender feels that making the short sale will cost it too much money, on the other hand, you simply won't get your deal done. If it feels a short sale is the cheapest (not to mention the quickest) way out, you will.

When You Have More Than One Mortgage

As we saw in Chapter 2, frequently people who are facing foreclosure have more than one mortgage on their property. They may have taken out a home equity loan, which is in the form of a second mortgage. And they may have taken out another loan in order to consolidate some credit card debt, which may be in the form of a third mortgage. And so on.

Additionally, they may have liens against the property. An auto loan was not paid, and the lender went to court and secured a judgment, which is now a lien against the property. There may be tax liens from the federal (IRS) and state governments. And so on.

Junior mortgage holders and lien holders can each put in their request for payment as part of the closing costs. But it's at the discretion of the lender of the first mortgage as to whether or not to allow it. Very frequently the first lender will simply shut out the others, refusing to pay almost anything. Thus lenders in junior positions (second, third, and so forth as well as many lien holders) will be wiped out and will get nothing or just a token payment.

Tax lien exceptions. The exception is if the lien holder is a state taxing body (such as one that collects property taxes). Their liens generally supersede any mortgage. Hence, the lender on the first mortgage must usually pay these in order to be able to get clear title back whether it's a short sale or a foreclosure.

It's Not How Much You Owe; It's How Much the Lender Will Forgive

Don't be intimidated by the amount of money by which you're under water. It really doesn't matter if it's $10,000 or $100,000 or $500,000. Regardless, if you need a short sale to sell, you may very well get it. Remember, you're not getting any cash out of a short sale. You're salvaging your credit. Thus the absolute amounts shouldn't matter to you.

Of course, they matter to a lender. But the lender is only concerned with mitigating loss. (That's why you'll be dealing with a loss mitigation committee.) You need to show a reasonable lender that it can lose less by doing a short sale than by going through foreclosure in order to get your deal. The rub, of course, is that some lenders just aren't reasonable and don't always do what's in their own best interests.

How Do I Find a Good Short Sale Agent?

You've checked it out (using the preliminary net sheet described in the last chapter) and you're under water and sinking fast. You need a short sale to bail you out. You think your best bet is to find an agent who can handle it for you. Where do you find that right agent?

In this chapter we'll examine the ins and outs of finding a good real estate agent to facilitate a short sale for you. But first, what about the cost of that agent? Given the high cost of sales commissions (between 4 and 6 percent, depending on where you live and how well you negotiate), the question of whether to handle the sale yourself or use an agent is one that most sellers wrestle with. Should you pay the commission, which can easily amount to $18,000 on a $300,000 sale, or should you save the money and sell it yourself?

That, however, is not the question for someone selling property as a short sale. Here it should be a no-brainer. After all, you're not paying the real estate commission; the foreclosing lender is. (If you're not sure how that works, reread Chapter 3.)

Why even bother to consider selling it on your own when you can, in effect, get the services of a broker for free? You get all the professional expertise of an agent, and someone else pays for it. (That makes sense, because with a short sale you're normally not getting any cash out of the deal; you're just saving your credit.) So why not simply hire an agent?

Actually, there are good reasons why you may want to handle your own short sale. Or, spend time carefully considering which agent to hire.

When Should I Sell It Myself and Save on Paying the Commission?

If you're wondering whether you can sell your property yourself and avoid paying a commission, the answer is that you can certainly try. And if the amount you are under water is only 5 or 6 percent of the anticipated sale price, then cutting out the commission might bring you to the surface. It may even allow you to get some cash out of the deal. Just keep in mind, however, that selling by yourself, particularly in today's market, is not going to be an easy chore. Indeed, it could prove to be very challenging. Check out the various "by owner" Web sites that offer help for the FSBO—for sale by owner—seller. These are some that I've found particularly useful:

www.owners.com
www.fsbo.com
www.forsalebyowner.com

Also, if you're only about 5 percent under water, check out the Obama housing plan for possible help in refinancing or loan modification. (See Chapter 7.)

When Lenders Were the Problem

It's important to get a handle on the overall short sale problem. As short a time as a year ago, even good agents had difficulty making short sales. The reason was the lenders themselves. Consider the following story.

Back in 2008 Singh wanted to sell his home using a short sale. His ARM (adjustable rate mortgage) had reset to a higher interest rate, and he couldn't afford the monthly payment. And, because he had bought the property at the height of the real estate bubble, its value had dropped by nearly half. He was deeply under water.

So he contacted a local agent. (I usually advise sellers to always use a local agent who is most likely to thoroughly understand the local market and who may have buyers ready to go for your property.) The local agent listed the home and within two months produced a buyer who was willing to pay market price, which was far below the amount that Singh owed.

A short sale agreement was drawn up, and Singh signed a letter authorizing his lender to deal directly with his agent. The agent presented the deal to the lender.

However, the lender was overwhelmed. It was set up to handle a few dozen foreclosures a month. Instead it had tens of thousands of them. It was using only three loan mitigation officers, and they didn't have the authority to close on a short sale without first taking the matter to the lender's board.

Thus Singh's short sale languished on a lending officer's desk for months until the foreclosure auction was held and Singh lost his home and his credit.

Whose fault was it? All blame was aimed at the lender, with much justification. The lender was unprepared to handle Singh's short sale, not to mention the thousands of others it faced.

When Agents Became the Problem

Times change, and so do the problems with getting a short sale. Now consider this story which occurred more recently. Dorothy owned a property right next door to Singh. She, too, had used an ARM to buy her home, and it had reset at a higher interest rate and monthly payment than she could afford. And her property also was worth only a fraction of its original price, and hence she was deeply under water.

So Dorothy, too, tried for a short sale. She hired the same real estate agent. He once again found a buyer, although this time there were so many foreclosures on the market that it took nearly five months. And by the time the sales agreement was drawn up, Dorothy was only weeks away from losing her home to a foreclosure auction.

The agent had Dorothy sign a sales agreement that included a short sale proposal and immediately sent it to the lender.

The proposal arrived on the loss mitigation committee desk of the lender on Tuesday. By Wednesday a worker had reviewed it and noted that the "package" was incomplete. There was no hardship letter explaining why Dorothy had to sell. There was no documentation of Dorothy's financial condition. There was no net sheet showing what the lender would net out. There was no appraisal of the property. And on and on.

The sales agreement and short sale proposal were bounced back to the agent with a terse note saying that it was incomplete. It included a list of documents the lender required.

The agent scratched his head. He'd been trying to work short sales for a year and thus far had not yet gotten one through. He blamed the lenders for their slowness and their lack of clarity.

He methodically began putting together a package of what he thought the lender wanted. It took the agent two weeks, and he sent it back in.

Again it was almost immediately bounced back by the lender with another terse note saying it was still incomplete; many of the forms were not the standard ones that the lender required. A list of the required forms was sent again to the agent.

The agent started over once again. But, you guessed it. Time ran out, and Dorothy's house, too, was sold at a foreclosure auction. (See Chapter 11 on beating the clock.)

Who's to Blame?

Notice the difference between the two attempts at short sales. In the case of Singh, it was apparently the lender's fault the short sale didn't go through. The lender was unprepared to handle short sales given the volume it had to deal with. It didn't have people or procedures in place.

By the time of the second instance, however, the lender had gotten its act together and was prepared. It had a loss mitigation committee. It knew which forms were needed. And it had people in authority ready to consider the short sale within one or two days of the proper package being submitted.

In the second case, it was mainly the agent's fault the deal did not go through. The agent was unfamiliar with the lender's procedures and requirements and failed to meet them. If he had, Dorothy might well have been able to sell her home. The agent was simply inexperienced when it came to handling a short sale.

MORAL

Although the biggest problem with short sales used to be lenders who were unprepared to handle them, since the beginning of 2009 most lenders (especially the bigger ones) have gotten their acts together. Today most are ready and able to deal with a short sale proposal on a fairly quick basis. Rather, it's the real estate agent who too often doesn't know what the lender needs and isn't able to put together a successful short sale package.

This is not to say that agents aren't trying. Many realize that this is a lucrative avenue of real estate sales and are moving into it.

Rather, it's simply to point out that times change and that it takes a while for people to catch up. The lenders had to catch up, and they did. Now the agents need to catch up, and I have every confidence that eventually they will. (The vast majority of agents are hardworking, dedicated salespeople devoted to helping their clients.)

However, if you're selling a home and need a short sale, then it would serve you well to carefully select your agent based on his or her knowledge and experience in dealing with lenders. Or, short sell it yourself.

How Do You Select a Good Short Sale Agent?

The criteria you use when selecting an agent should include all the usual elements, which we consider at the end of this chapter, *plus* a few extras that are important to the success of your short sale. Those special extras in the form of questions to ask the agent appear in the following passages.

Extra Question No. 1: Are You Experienced in Short Sales?

What you need to do is to establish the experience of your agent in the area of short sales—the area of your immediate concern. Lately, since short sales have become such a big part of real estate, a lot of agents have tried to become instant experts. However, trying doesn't make it so.

Listen to what the agent says. Most are honest and up front. If she tells you that she hasn't done any short sales at all, then thank that agent for her honesty, but my suggestion is for you to move on. You don't want to have an agent learning on your time, particularly when the clock to foreclosure is ticking down.

If the agent says that he's done a few short sales, which I take to mean one or two but no more, my suggestion is that you reread the paragraph above. A few is better than none, but he's still a beginner. Again, you're probably dealing with an inexperienced agent.

On the other hand, if the agent says that she's worked on many, dozens, more than dozens, then you may actually be barking up the right tree. If the agent is being candid, then you may have found your expert. One agent I know was doing short sales even during the housing bubble of five years ago. When the market turned, it was like the happy hunting ground of real estate sales suddenly appeared before her.

Extra Question No. 2: What Is Your Success Ratio?

Working on short sales doesn't mean actually concluding them successfully. The agent could be like the one in our example above, still trying to come up with that first elusive short sale.

My experience is that most agents will simply tell you the truth. "I've never closed one." Or, "I've only closed a couple." Or, if you're lucky, "I've closed dozens."

Some agents will give you a percentage. "I've closed about 10 percent." Or, "I've closed about 30 percent." Or, one agent who claimed, "I've closed about 80 percent." (It turned out he had, but had only done four or five short sale transactions.)

I'd go with an agent who had successfully closed many short sales and who had a higher percentage of success. But, then I'd ask the final and perhaps most important question, which follows.

Extra Question No. 3: Can You Give Me a List of Successful Short Sale Sellers You've Handled Whom I Can Call for a Reference?

This is where the rubber meets the road, where push comes to shove, where the truth comes out. If the agent can hand you a list of, say, 10 sellers for whom she's successfully handled short sales, you've got a live one. But, of course, *check the references.* Anyone can prepare a list from a phone book.

Talk to the successful sellers and ask them if they were satisfied with the agent. Ask the all-important question of them: "Would you use this agent again?"

Get some good recommendations and you've probably found your good agent. (But read on for other concerns.)

On the other hand, keep an open mind if your agent says something like, "I'm not sure I can give you a list. After all, these are sellers who were facing foreclosure. They may simply not want to talk about their financial situation."

It's true. In the course of writing this book, I found it as hard as pulling teeth to get successful short sale sellers to talk with me. Most were embarrassed by their financial experience and simply wanted to put it behind them.

Even so, the agent should be able to give you the MLS (Multiple Listing Service) numbers of the properties sold. He or she should be able to pull up the old listings on the computer, which should indicate whether or not the property was eventually sold and if your agent was the seller's agent or buyer's agent, or both (see below for discussion of dual agency).

Furthermore, the agent should be able to produce at least a couple of names and numbers. Some people will talk simply out of a desire to help someone else who is now in a position they were in. Thus, any successful short sale agent should be able to at least get a couple of sellers who are willing to discuss things with you. If necessary, have the agent call them first and ask permission. You'll probably get a chance to speak with them.

When You Don't Get a Good Agent

This is Mark's story. He was selling a home and asked the questions noted above until he found an experienced short sale agent, one who had done many deals and who knew where the lender mitigation committees were and what to put into their packages.

So he hired Ted.

Ted put Mark's house on the MLS that Realtors use to co-broke properties. He priced it at market value, which was at least $100,000 less than Ted owed.

It took a couple of months, but Ted found two buyers. The first buyer was an investor who low-balled the price, coming in $50,000 less than asking. The second buyer wanted to occupy the property. She had cash and wanted to offer the full price.

But the second buyer, Sally, was savvy about real estate. She said that since Ted was going to represent both buyer and seller, he'd get a full commission of 5 or 6 percent. She wanted him to fork over 1 percent to her. After all, she said, it was a rich sale since he represented both parties, and it was fairly simple since she was offering cash without anyone having to worry about getting any difficult financing. Besides, in today's tough market most agents were discounting their commissions. Why should she pay Ted more?

Ted flat out refused. Instead, he said he'd get the lender to give her back up to 3 percent of her closing costs. He said he knew the lender was doing that on such deals.

Sally said thank you, but insisted on the 1 percent. If the lender was offering 3 percent back for closing costs, that was between her and the lender. She said that the deal with the lender was separate from the deal with Ted. She insisted on her 1 percent discount.

Ted became quite angry and accused Sally of unethical conduct. Sally looked surprised and confused. "What's unethical about asking for a discount on a rich commission?" she asked.

Ted said he already had another offer to take to the seller, and he refused to take hers. He left in a huff.

So Sally went to a discount broker to make the offer. (Many discount brokers regularly offer a portion of their commission to the buyer. ZipRealty.com, for example, offers 20 percent of its commission to a buyer who makes an offer and purchases the property.)

The discount broker wrote up the offer and presented it to Ted, the listing agent, who said he'd take care of it.

Now we switch back to Mark, the seller. Ted presented him with one offer, the one for $50,000 less than the asking price. He never presented him with Sally's offer.

Since it was the only one, Mark took it and Ted presented it to the lender, who subsequently rejected it because it was too low. The house remained unsold, and the clock was ticking.

Sally never heard one way or the other about her offer. She called her discount broker who said he had called, e-mailed, and faxed Ted, all to no avail. Eventually Sally called Mark directly, which was the first time he'd heard about her offer.

However, by then it was too late. The foreclosure auction was upon them, Mark lost his home, and Sally never bought it.

MORAL

While it's important to get an agent who is savvy about short sales, you also want an agent who's scrupulously honest and who always serves you. Some agents actually get between you and a deal because they're greedy.

In this example, Ted betrayed his fiduciary relationship to Mark by not presenting Sally's offer. Agents are supposed to present offers as they come in, not hold any back and not wait until the first has been rejected to present the second. If Mark had pursued the matter, Ted might have had his license jeopardized, even be legally liable. As it was, Mark simply slunk away after the foreclosure auction, too worn out by the whole process to really care.

What could Mark have done? He could have insisted that Ted present all offers immediately. He could have been wary. After all, Sally came to see the house several times and told him directly she was going to make a good offer. Where was it?

What could Sally have done? She might have written up her offer with a clause insisting that her discount broker be on hand when it was presented to the seller, Mark. In some states such a demand in an offer must be honored by the listing agent.

The best thing that could have been done, however, was for Mark to get an agent who not only specialized in short sales but also was scrupulously honest, diligent, and, most important, loyal to him.

The Basics to Look For in an Agent

We've covered the extras that you want in a short sale agent—those that show that he or she knows and understands the process. Now here are the basics that you should look for in *any* agent.

Where Can I Find a Top-Notch Agent?

Ask your friends if they know people who have recently sold their home. There are so many agents around (close to 1 percent of the population in some areas) that almost everyone knows one. Did the sellers have a good experience? Ask them if they would use the agent again. Ask them if they have any reservations about the agent.

Finding any old agent is easy. Just put a FSBO (for sale by owner pronounced "fisbo") sign on your front lawn. You'll have agents climbing all over you trying to get your listing. Finding a *good* agent, however, is a bit more challenging. I suggest you pick a real estate office that's nearby (being close is important because, presumably, the agents will know the immediate area well) and check it out.

Don't ask to see the agent who's "up." Ask to see the broker. Then ask how many of its *own listings* this office has sold in the past six months. The broker should know exactly. If the agents haven't sold any, or there's any hemming and hawing, leave.

Along the way, listen carefully to what the broker says. Is there one name, one agent, who keeps popping up? Is that agent, in fact, the best seller in the office?

At the end of your brief discussion, ask the broker who is the best seller in the office in terms of sales (not listings) made. Most brokers will chuckle at your audacity but will also probably give you a straight answer. (Is it the same name that kept popping up in your earlier conversation?)

Interview the Agent

While knowing that the agent is a great salesperson is an enormous plus for you, you also need to know something more about him or her (in addition to the questions noted above about specific experience in short sales). You want to be sure the person is competent in the real estate business in general, is honest in dealings, and is reliable. You should ask the agent the following questions:

1. **How long have you been in the real estate business?**
   The learning curve for real estate is fairly long. The reason is that the number of transactions a person can become involved with at any one time is limited. Usually it takes 3 to 5 years for an agent to have gotten a well-rounded education; 5 to 10 years is better.
2. **What professional organizations do you belong to?**
   The minimum here should be the local real estate board and Multiple Listing Service (MLS), as well as the state association and National Association of Realtors (NAR). The agent may also be a member of the chamber of commerce and local citizens' groups—all pluses.

3. **What will you do to expedite the short sale of my home?**

   The answer should be immediate, direct, and comprehensive. The agent should explain an action plan that he or she hopes will sell your house. The plan should include:

   A. Getting a buyer during a limited listing time frame. (Beware of agents who want to list for more than three months; you can always extend the listing later. But, if they do a poor job, you're locked in for the term.)

   B. Promotion, including talking up the listing at the local real estate board.

   C. Advertising.

   D. Open houses.

4. **May I see your license?**

   Agents in all states are required to be licensed and to display that license. If you see that they are operating under a suspended or restricted license, you certainly would want to know why. And you ought to evaluate their explanation carefully.

5. **Are you full time or part time?**

   Many agents do real estate sales on a part-time basis. Some are retired from other professions (teaching, the military, corporations, and so on) and sell real estate part time as a way of supplementing their pensions.

   There's nothing at all wrong with this. However, my own experience is that many part-time salespeople aren't on top of things. They don't devote the full-time effort that's needed to get things done, especially selling in a tough market.

6. **Will you negotiate on the commission?**

   It's a critical point. As we saw above, an agent who was inflexible can mess up a deal. While a good agent may want a full commission, he or she won't let it get in the way of making a good deal for you.

7. **How will you evaluate my house?**

Any agent worth his or her salt will provide you with a complete CMA (comparative market analysis) of your home. It will show both the price of comparable homes currently for sale as well as what recent comparables sold for. (You can ask if the agent will provide you with a CMA—leave if he or she won't or doesn't know what you're talking about.)

However, really good local agents will know neighborhoods and streets. Tell them where you live and right away they should have a good idea of what your house is worth.

Does meeting this criterion (or missing it) prove that the agent is good (or bad)? No, not necessarily. But, I'd feel a whole lot better with an agent who was so familiar with my neighborhood that he or she knew price values without having to look them up.

8. **What do you think of the other agents in this town?**

This is a final trick question that I suggest you ask. (You can substitute the name of a specific agent, if you know one.) Agents who have been around for a while know just about all the other agents in town. Therefore, a good agent should say something like, "Sure, I know so and so."

Then listen to what the agent says next. Does he knock the other agent and say something like, "She's terrible, got lots of clients in trouble, doesn't know how to make a deal"? Or does he simply let things pass saying something like, "I hear she does a pretty good job."

My own feeling is that I would never hire an agent who knocks another. It shows a lack of professionalism, and it's immature. And if this person knocks another agent, what will she or he say *or do* about you?

Should I Go with a Chain or an Independent Office?

Twenty or thirty years ago virtually all real estate agents were independent. Today, the vast majority belong to a national chain such as Century 21, RE/MAX, Coldwell Banker, Prudential, or some other national company. These are big names and big companies.

Thus, one of the first questions that most sellers ask is: Should I go with a chain or with an independent?

The answer is that the question is often irrelevant. One of the best tips this book can give you is that you should go with the best agent you can find. If that agent happens to be associated with a chain, great. If the agent is independent, just as great. Don't base your listing decision solely on the sign in front of the office. Remember, it's your agent who will ultimately make, or not make, the deal and on whose advice you will be relying.

Will the Agent Negotiate on the Commission?

Even many experienced sellers aren't aware that commissions and listings are fully negotiable. They just assume that there's a going rate and that the agent will give them that. Nothing could be further from the truth. There is no "going rate," and every agent should negotiate for the listing terms, conditions, and commission rate. In our above example we saw the trouble that can come from an agent who won't consider negotiating a commission rate.

Keep in mind that it is both illegal and unethical in all areas of the country for a real estate board to "set" a standard rate of commission, so don't accept that excuse. Commissions today range from a low flat rate of about $400 to a high of 3 percent of the selling price going to the listing office. Of course, there's also the amount that goes to the office that brings in a buyer. That is typically anywhere from 2 to 3 percent. Thus the total commission runs the gamut from about 2.5 percent plus $400 to a total of 6 percent of the selling price.

Of course, if you're going with a short sale, the lender ultimately has to approve the commission rate. Nevertheless, knowing that your agent will negotiate the commission means that you can feel comfortable that he or she won't let it get in the way of a deal.

Understanding the Listing Agreement

Finally there's the matter of the listing agreement. You'll need to agree to its terms in order for the agent to list your house.

Be careful. In some cases you might owe a commission, even if your house doesn't sell, even if the lender refuses to accept a short sale! Read the agreement carefully. Take it to your attorney. Know what you are signing!

There is a variety of listing types an agent can offer you. (No, there isn't just one standard listing agreement that they all use.) Each type of listing has its own pluses and minuses and should be considered in light of your specific short sale needs. The listing agreement will normally say right on the face the type that it is. You can negotiate the type of listing agreement with the agent.

Exclusive Right to Sell

An exclusive right-to-sell listing is the type that almost all agents prefer. I prefer it as well as a seller for a short sale.

It means that if the agent or anyone else (including you) sells the house, you owe the agent a commission. Even if you sell the house on your own to someone who saw it while it was listed, for a certain period of time after the listing expires (typically a few months) you could still owe the commission.

In other words, with this type of listing you ensure the agent a commission if the house is sold. The only way the agent cannot get a commission is if there is no sale. Sellers tend to dislike this type of commission because they feel it's unfair—especially if they produce a buyer on their own.

Agents, on the other hand, like it because they feel protected. Most are willing to put forth 100 percent effort only if they get this type of listing. Otherwise, they're afraid a buyer and seller will get together behind the agent's back and cheat the agent out of a commission. As I said, this is the most common type of listing used, one that I would use for a short sale.

Exclusive Agency

With an exclusive agency, if the agent sells the house, you owe a commission. If you sell it to someone the agent didn't show it to, you don't owe anything. You may be thinking that this is a listing that's more to your liking.

This type of listing also has its pluses and minuses. Agents have good reasons for not liking this type of listing. They may bring buyers to your home who tell them they're not interested in purchasing. Later, the buyers come to you and negotiate a sale. You claim no commission is due because you had no knowledge that the agent showed these buyers the home; they dealt directly with you. The agent claims that a commission is due because he or she found the buyer.

In this case, the agent is right. But to get that commission the agent might have to go to arbitration or even to court. Along the way there's sure to be hard feelings, and agents are very concerned about their reputation in a community. Furthermore, when a lender is involved as in a short sale, it gets even more complicated. The lender may simply bow out of the deal to avoid any potential lawsuits involving the agent. In other words, it could cost you the deal.

An exclusive agency listing is sometimes appropriately used when you have a buyer or buyers who you think might be interested in purchasing, but who haven't yet committed. You want to list the property and get it onto the market, but you want to exclude paying a commission for those buyers you've already found.

With a short sale, I wouldn't play around with this type of listing.

Open Listing

With an open listing, you agree to pay a commission to any broker who brings you a buyer or to pay no commission if you find the buyer. You might simply let every agent know that the property is for sale and that you'll pay a commission, but you're not willing to give any one of them an "exclusive."

Some sellers think this is a good type of listing, because you can give it to any agent.

Most agents, however, won't devote 10 minutes of time to this kind of listing. If buyers should show up whom the agents can't interest in any other piece of property, then they'll bring them to you in a last-chance effort at a commission. The opportunity to do work and not get paid for it is so great here that agents in general just don't want to bother with this type of listing.

About the only time it's used is in bare land, when the chances of selling are very slim and it could take years to produce a buyer.

If you want to sell short, I wouldn't suggest using this type of listing. You won't get many agents willing to spend the time and energy needed to pull off the short sale without being guaranteed a commission, such as the above listings offer.

Guaranteed-Sale Listing

I mention a guaranteed-sale listing and the following net listing because you just might (although it is unlikely) come across them. A guaranteed-sale listing isn't a separate type of listing. Rather it's any of the above but is usually the exclusive right to sell. The listing simply includes a separate clause that says that if the property isn't sold by the end of the listing term, then the agent agrees to buy it from you for a set price (usually the listing price or lower), less the commission.

Although widely used at one time, this type of listing is almost never used in a short sale. There are simply too many unknowns when dealing with a lender and too many opportunities to have conflicts of interest. Besides, it may be almost impossible for an agent to get the financing needed to buy your property.

If an agent does suggest it, you should wonder if there's some scam at play about the property sale that you didn't know. Is there a buyer hiding in the wings ready to pay a whole lot more than you're asking? More than you owe? Is there a "straw man" deal involved? (See Chapter 13.)

Be careful with a guaranteed-sale listing. It's almost too good to be true. And may well be.

Net Listing

In a net listing you agree up front on a fixed price for the property. Everything over that price goes to the agent.

When you owe more than your home is worth, I cannot imagine an agent asking for a net listing. It simply wouldn't make sense. The easiest way to handle a net listing is to simply avoid it.

The Listing Agreement

The listing agreement is often several pages long and may contain a considerable amount of legalese. (It's always a good idea to have your attorney check it out.) However, there are a number of points that it should contain and that you should watch out for:

1. **Price.** The listing agreement should specify the price you expect to receive for your property.

2. **Deposit.** The agreement should indicate how large a deposit you expect from a buyer. It should also indicate that the agent may hold the deposit but that it is your money. Usually such agreements specify that if the buyer doesn't go through with the deal, you and the agent split the deposit. In a short sale, however, the agent sometimes holds the buyer's uncashed check until the lender accepts the offer.

3. **Terms.** It's important that the terms you are willing to accept are spelled out. Since it's a short sale, the agreement should specify this. It should say that there's no sale without lender approval. In actual practice, that doesn't preclude an agent from bringing you a buyer who offers other terms. It just means you don't have to accept such a buyer. Be sure that the terms spell out exactly what you're looking for in a short sale. Remember, you don't want to be liable for a commission when the agent produces a buyer "ready, willing, and able" to purchase. You want the commission tied to a lender's acceptance of a short sale and the close of escrow.

4. **Multiple Listing Service.** The fastest way to get your home sold is to be sure it's on the MLS. The listing should specify that the agent will place it on the MLS. (Doing so actually costs the agent a few bucks.) Typically only agents who are Realtors can list on the MLS.

5. **Title insurance.** Today almost all property sold has title insurance. The only questions are which title company to use and who is going to pay for it. The listing agreement usually specifies both. In most areas title insurance costs are split between buyer and seller, although in some states the seller pays them. If it's a short sale, the lender will

often determine the title insurance company to be used
and allow for the insurance out of the buyer's funds.

6. **Key box.** Buyers come by when they're ready, not when
you're ready. Therefore, it's a good idea to allow the agent
to show the property even when you're not home. Since
there may be many cooperative agents, the common way of
handling this is to have a key box installed. The listing agreement asks you to give permission for a key box. Be aware,
however, that you are opening your home up to a great
many people. Agents and buyers represent a broad spec-
trum of people. Just as in the general population, there are
those who are scrupulously honest as well as those who are
dishonest in real estate. While the incidence of theft from
homes with key boxes installed is small, robbery does occasionally occur. Therefore, for the time you have a key box
on your home and while you are still residing there, you are
well advised to remove all valuables. *Note:* In many listing
agreements the agents specifically disclaim responsibility for
loss resulting from having a key box improperly used.

7. **Sign.** You should give permission for the agent to install a
reasonable sign in your front yard. It's an excellent method
of attracting buyers, perhaps the best.

8. **Arbitration and attorney's fees.** Typically these agreements
call for arbitration in case of a dispute and state that in the
case of a lawsuit the prevailing party will have his or her
attorney's costs paid by the losing party. Read this wording
carefully. You may want to ask an attorney if you should
sign or change it.

9. **Disclosure.** The listing agreement should also list the various disclosures that you as a seller must make to a buyer
in your state. In many states the agent is likewise required
to make an inspection of the property and disclose any
defects he or she finds.

10. **Equal housing disclosure.** You must be in compliance with federal and state antidiscrimination laws when you list your property.

11. **Beginning and expiration dates.** Perhaps the most critical part of the document is the clause that states when the listing you are giving expires. It should be a written-out date—"June 1, 2010"—and should not say something like "in three months." If the date isn't inserted, the agent could insist that you did intend the listing to be renewable every three months. I suggest never giving a listing for more than three months. In most markets that should be enough time for you to determine how good the agent really is. If there are extenuating circumstances, at the end of the three-month period, you might want to extend the listing for an additional three months. Or you might want to secure the services of a different agent.

12. **Commission.** The agreement will state the percentage of commission that you've agreed upon. Beware of a clause right next to it that may state something to the effect that if you take your house off the market for any reason, you owe the agent a fee that is then written in. This is a "liquidated damages" clause, and it means that although you may not have to pay the full commission if you decide not to sell, you are committing yourself to paying something, often a substantial amount of money. (Have your attorney check this out.)

    With a short sale, if for some reason you suddenly discover you've inherited some money or won the lottery, you may be able to keep your house and want to pull it off the market. You don't want to be liable for a commission if you do so.

    Further, as noted above, be sure that the commission is to be paid only upon completion of the sale. Simply

bringing in a buyer who is ready, willing, and able to purchase—the standard criteria for earning a commission—
won't work when there's a short sale for which you need
lender approval.

In addition to the listing agreement itself, most agents
will provide you with an agent's disclosure document stat-
ing whether the agent is a seller's agent, a buyer's agent, or
a dual agent. (See "Buyer's Agents vs. Seller's Agents.)

13. **Back-out clause.** Back-out clauses aren't normally in listings; however, because of your short sale circumstances,
you may want one. Basically, it says that you can withdraw
the listing usually if some specific event occurs. For example, say you find you can do a deal with a buyer whom the
lender will approve, providing no commission (or a lesser
one) is paid. In other words, the only thing standing
between your getting out from under water is the agent's
commission. The buyer won't pay more. The lender won't
take less. A back-out clause allows you to back out of the
listing and make the deal.

Some states have rules that a real estate agent cannot
get in the way of a deal. Of course, that does not include
circumstances in which the buyer or seller are simply trying to evade paying an earned commission. However, in a
short sale, sometimes the only way to make the deal is to
cut the commission or, in an extreme case, eliminate it.
The agent should not prevent you from getting out from
under.

14. **Transaction fee.** This is a fee that brokers have been tacking
on that is paid directly to their office. It's often around
$500. It's over and above the commission.

Brokers charge this fee because they are paying their
salespeople higher commissions, leaving less for their over-
head. However, that's their problem, not yours. I wouldn't

sign any listing with a transaction fee in it. Foreclosing lenders probably won't pay it. And you don't want to be liable for it.

Listing Danger Signals

Here are some red flags you want to look for when listing your property for a short sale:

1. Agent wants listing for more than three months.
2. Agent insists on a commission higher than you want to pay.
3. Agent insists on the commission being paid when a buyer is produced, not when the deal closes, even if the lender refuses a short sale.
4. Agent pressures you to sign. (If brokers pressure you to sign the listing, think what they'll do when a bad offer comes in.)
5. Agent hedges on the disclosures, saying that you don't really need to disclose a major defect to the buyer or the lender. Doing this can get you in real trouble.
6. Agent doesn't want to allow you a back-out clause, even though he or she understands the property is being sold on a short sale.

What the Agent Owes You

If I agree to list, what does the agent owe me in return?

Giving a listing on your home for sale is not a one-way street. The agent also agrees to give you something in return. That something includes the following.

The Agent Owes You

Service

Loyalty

Diligence

Honesty

Disclosure of facts

Skill

Care

Some of the above may actually be stated in the listing agreement. Others are considered part of the agent's fiduciary responsibilities. All are considered examples of ethical conduct.

Buyer's Agents vs. Seller's Agents

As noted above, when you list with an agent, he or she owes you loyalty. That takes many forms. It means that you can rely on the agent's good advice during the transaction.

Why should the agent be loyal to you and not to the buyer?

The Seller's Agent

The reason the agent should be loyal to you, the seller, has to do with the agent's fiduciary (position of trust) relationship with you. It is incumbent upon the agent to tell you any fact that may help you in making your decision to sell. In other words, the agent is bound to you in ways that are definitely to your advantage.

TIP

It's important not to get too smug about agent relationships. Not all agents stick to the letter of ethical conduct, and some agents (buyer's agents) may have fiduciary responsibilities to the buyers and not to you.

The Buyer's Agent

Thus far we've talked about a seller's agent, the one who takes your listing. However, today many agents work for the buyer. They may even have the buyer sign an agreement like a listing. As a seller, be wary of buyer's agents. They do not owe to you the same fiduciary responsibility as do seller's agents. Indeed, their responsibilities are reversed. They owe them to the buyers!

TIP

Whether an agent represents a buyer or a seller depends on who the agent declares for. Who pays the agent—you, the lender, or the buyer—is not the issue. In fact, it's common for the seller's (your) agent to split the commission with the buyer's agent, so in effect, in a traditional sale, you, the seller, are paying the buyer's agent!

What Are Dual Agents?

A dual agent is one who not only works for you, the seller, but also works for the buyer. The dual agent represents both parties—there's only one agent for both buyer and seller.

Nevertheless, the agent must disclose who he or she works for—you, the buyer, or both. Agents must offer disclosure. And it should be in writing.

Which Type of Agent Do You Want?

Obviously, as a seller you're not going to want a buyer's agent. But what about a seller's agent versus a dual agent?

The answer should be straightforward. When you're selling your house, you want only a seller's agent. You want to be sure that the person with whom you list will represent you thoroughly.

That's all well and good. But what happens when your agent goes out and brings in a buyer (no other agent involved)? Does your agent now become a *dual* agent?

Maybe. It all comes out in disclosure. The agent who brings you the offer on your house should disclose what type of agent she or he is. If he or she doesn't disclose, you should demand a disclosure.

Whenever an offer is presented, demand to know who the agent presenting the offer represents. The agent should tell you. If the agent doesn't, assume that person is acting for the buyer, and treat the offer adversarially. The point to understand is that the agent determines whom she or he represents. Your goal is to find out who it is and then act accordingly. It's like what the referee tells boxers in a prizefight: "Always protect yourself."

Preparing Your Home to Show When You're Not Going to Net a Dime

Why on earth should you spend 10 cents on your house when, in a short sale, you're going to net zero out of it?

That's the question that every short sale seller asks. And how you answer could make the difference between selling your home and salvaging your credit, or facing a foreclosure on your credit report for the next 7 to 10 years.

I've visited many homes offered as short sales. If the sellers happen still to be present on the property, they tend to have made a mess. (Very often the sellers have moved out, which can be another problem.) The resident owners know that one way or another they are going to have to leave, so often they have packing boxes strewn about. There are clothes draped over furniture, and the kitchen and bathroom countertops are covered with items ready to be packed away. In some cases it's even hard to walk through the home.

And, because so many of their possessions are out, these sellers want to be around when potential buyers come by to be sure that nobody walks off with something. And they project negativism. They know they are losing their homes, so they tend to be morose, unsmiling, and uncooperative.

Of course, in a short sale it's about the money, and sometimes buyers are investors who can see through all this. But many times the would-be buyers are planning to live in the homes themselves. And what they see is a big turnoff.

If ever there was an example of how *not* to show a home for sale, it would undoubtedly come from a seller who's still living on the property and trying to go short. Typically the most promising buyer can't wait to get away. Buyers run, not walk, from the house. And if they do make an offer, it's to lowball.

Of course, since the sellers aren't getting anything out of the sale, why should they care if it's a lowball or not?

The reason is that the lender is far less likely to accept a lowball offer than a more reasonable one that's closer to market price. The bottom line on this is that most short sale sellers shoot themselves in the foot by the way they present their homes, especially when they're still living in them.

They've given up. And in so doing, they may be condemning themselves to 7 to 10 years of bad credit reports.

The Savvy Seller

On the other hand, there are the savvy short sale sellers who realize what's at stake. And they properly prepare their house for showing.

Just like anything else you want to sell, in order to get an offer at the best price, you have to show it off at its best. In the trade, agents sometimes refer to such properties as "doll houses" or say that they "show well."

When buyers walk through, they are impressed. They can see themselves living there. They want to make the best offer they can, just to be sure that someone else, who's also likely to be impressed, doesn't beat them out of the home.

If you're selling a home that you have equity in, I always advise spending a few weeks cleaning and refurbishing. This may include repainting large portions of the property, fixing broken screens and doors, even replacing the carpeting. It wasn't uncommon in better times for sellers to spend upwards of $5,000 to $10,000 staging their homes for sale.

Of course, when you're trying to sell your home short, that's ridiculous. It would be throwing good money after bad. It would be fixing up a house that you're, essentially, giving away.

So, how much, if anything, should you spend preparing your home for a short sale? What should you do to entice a looker to become a buyer who makes a good offer? What makes sense, and what doesn't?

Things You Should Do

My limit in terms of what to spend is $50. Is it worth 50 bucks to save your credit? I think so. And a few years down the road when you want to buy another home, you probably will think so, too. The following provides advice on what you should do.

Declutter—Cost $0.00

Even if you're not packing to move, most buyers will probably see your normal furniture as cluttered. After all, they're trying to visualize how their furniture, clothing, and other things will look in the house. How can they do it when your things are packed in there?

So here's what you should do. Get rid of your excess stuff. Store it, sell it, dump it. Do so, and buyers will think your home is just right.

Of course, if you are packing, then the least you can do is to designate a particular area of the house where all the packing boxes go. It could be an unused bedroom, the garage, or, in good weather, even the back deck. Normally, I tell sellers not to do this, to get all their excess stuff off the property. But in an extreme case when you're facing foreclosure and need a short sale, buyers will be a bit more understanding. And you can use a place on the premises for storage.

Basically what you then have to do is to declutter each room and make it presentable. Here are some guidelines for decluttering:

- **Be sure to keep things off countertops.** Remove pots, pans, old food, and anything else from kitchen surfaces. Clean out the sink and at the least put the dirty dishes and knives and forks in the dishwasher. Store everything else in the cabinets. Simply make the kitchen and baths look neat.
- **Remove extra furniture.** One double or queen-sized bed in a bedroom is maximum. One table and set of chairs in a dining room. No cluttered chairs or couches in the living or family room. No rugs on top of rugs. After all, you're going to be moving anyhow—just get rid of the extra stuff, now.
- **Remove any clothes from sight.** Clothes that are not in drawers should be neatly hung in closets. Most of us have too many clothes in our closets, making them look small. Try to box up and remove excess clothing.
- **Remove toys.** Don't have them scattered on the floor, but neatly put them away in drawers or boxes. When buyers walk through the house, they should be able to navigate through the rooms without the threat of tripping over your children's things.

Just take part of a weekend and straighten up your house. Get rid of any items that would get in the way of a buyer's appreciation of it.

Cleanup—Cost $0.00 (Detergent and Other Cleaners—Cost $10)

Cleaning is different from decluttering. Clean means washing the countertops, not just taking stuff off of them. Yes, it's a pain, but just think of it as if you were entertaining every weekend. You'd clean all the countertops, the sinks, the toilets, and the tub and shower. You'd vacuum the carpet and occasionally wash the windows. Pick half a day each week and do it. Once you get things clean, the next pass will go faster and be easier.

A word about carpets. Normally I suggest that sellers have them professionally cleaned, which can cost a couple of hundred dollars. If they really want to make their home look terrific, they can replace them with inexpensive new carpeting. But, that can cost $5,000 more or less at minimum.

However, you're facing a short sale. You don't want to spend any money you're not going to get back and which you may desperately need elsewhere. So forget about professional cleaning and replacing. Instead, vacuum thoroughly. (You do have a vacuum cleaner, don't you? If not, borrow one from a neighbor.)

Where there are spots, use a spot remover. I use Resolve. It costs about $7 and usually works pretty well. Once you get your carpet cleaned up, keep it that way. It doesn't take that long to vacuum once a week.

Cut and Trim—Cost $0.00 (Hauling Junk to the Dump $10.00)

Start with cleaning the outside. Driveway cleaning can come down to something as simple as using some detergent and hosing down the surface. Do the same for walkways.

Mow the lawn and trim the shrubs. You can probably get by with mowing once every couple of weeks. The shrubs may not need much more than a trim once a month.

Be sure to remove the trash that tends to accumulate at the side of your house. It looks bad and can prevent proper drainage, which in wet weather can turn your backyard into a swamp—something that's very likely to put off buyers.

Clean the door handles of the house. They're very important because they are something that buyers typically look at closely.

Paint—Cost $40.00

Paint (or restain) the front door of your house. It will go a long way toward brightening up the place.

Paint any interior walls that are badly marked up. (It's often easier to paint a wall than to try and clean it.) Touch up everywhere else. (Make sure you use exactly the same color and paint type to touch up, or your work will itself need touching up!)

Do not paint ceilings, unless they have a serious spotting problem. Do not paint all the walls—just the ones in bad shape. Do paint in kitchens and baths where paint is chipping, peeling, or otherwise looks bad.

Fix—Cost $?.00

If something is broken, it should be fixed. Except when it's a short sale and especially except for big ticket items. Simply disclose that it's broken. The buyer will take it off the price. So will the lender. (Make sure it's on your net sheet to the lender so it will allow a fix-up discount.)

The following are some big ticket items:

- Roof
- Hot-water heater

- Furnace/air conditioner
- Structure
- Foundation
- Flooring
- Counters
- Mold removal
- Appliances that go with the house

If something is a safety issue, such as a broken light switch, you probably should fix it for your own well being, if you're living in the house. If you don't fix it, be sure to disclose it.

Other small items, such as a broken door hinge or handle or a leaking faucet, you may want to fix yourself simply because it's usually easy to do and costs virtually nothing, and not fixing it means you're creating a nuisance.

Bottom Line

It shouldn't cost you more than 50 bucks to put your home in shape. Plus, of course, a weekend or maybe two of elbow grease.

Is it worthwhile? It will be if you sell your home and salvage your credit.

Things You Should *Not* Do

Following are some suggested don'ts. Most are self-evident, but some people do the strangest things.

Remodeling of Any Kind

Don't do any remodeling. This should go without saying, yet I've met short sale sellers who are in the process of remodeling a kitchen or a bath, or in one instance, actually adding a bathroom!

Why, I asked, would you spend the time and money to do any kind of work on a home that you're not going to net any money out of? Every dime you put in is automatically lost.

The most common answer is that they started the project before they got into trouble (before the loan reset, or they lost their job, or got a divorce, or whatever). Now they simply have a need to complete.

Ignore the need. Stop the project. Let the buyer figure out how much it's going to cost him or her to complete the job, and let the lender take it off the loan. Stop thinking of it as your home. Your home is going to be the next place you move into.

Carpet Replacement

I don't care how bad the carpet looks; don't spend a dime replacing it. If it's torn and full of spots, smells of animal odors and is thoroughly noxious, take it up and leave the subfloor. But don't you dare spend a dime on new carpeting that you won't enjoy and that you won't get a dime back for.

Major Repairs

This is not the time for repairing the furnace, or the water heater, or even the garbage disposal. If you're in the house, live with it. Let the next buyer and the lender work out who'll pay for it.

Spend Money on the House

Soon it's not going to be your house. In a short sale you won't get any of your money back. And everyone will rightly think you foolish for spending money on it.

When the House Is Empty

Most of the short sale properties I look at are empty. The sellers have already moved out and moved on.

However, the ones that are likely to sell are neat and clean. In some, the sellers have left a little furniture to give at least a couple of rooms a lived-in look. It helps buyers to envision where a bed, a table, or a couch might go. But most are totally empty.

After you leave, try to paint out any spots on walls. Clean bathrooms and the kitchen thoroughly. Sweep and vacuum every room.

Most important, don't leave boxes and other junk lying around. That's a complete turnoff for buyers. They will suspect that you resent moving (which you very well may) and are going to be difficult to deal with in a transaction (which may not be the case). Don't buy into buyers' worst fears.

Clean up and clear out. It will make selling your home much easier.

How to Talk to a Lender

I t was only a year or two ago that talking to a fore-closing lender about a short sale or an REO (real estate owned)—property taken over through foreclosure—was almost impossible. Foreclosing lenders wouldn't even admit that they had problem loans or that they had taken over any properties. I guess they were afraid the public in general might get the wrong idea, that they had made a couple of bad loans.

How times change. Today you can go to almost any major lender's Web site and be directed to its REO properties. Some of the bigger ones have tens of thousands of properties they hold after foreclosing; some hundreds of thousands!

And it's no longer a big deal contacting them about a short sale. You don't tend to get surprised secretaries trying to figure out what you're talking about. Just mention short sale, loan workout, or loss mitigation and very likely you'll quickly find yourself talk-ing to the right people.

Of course, that doesn't mean that once you get to the right person it's an easy conversation. Lender negotiators, facilitators, mitigation officers, or whatever your lender happens to call its short sale employees are busy. *Harried* would probably be the right word. When you finally do get through, they'll usually answer any direct questions you have, but most are not willing to do much hand holding. State your business, and get on with it. They just don't have a lot of time to chat. (See the list of loan mitigation phone numbers for major lenders at the end of this chapter.)

So, just what do you want from these people?

Questions to Ask

If you're not looking for a loan modification (see Chapter 7), then you want only one thing—to get a short sale. Therefore, your questions should be brief so they can be answered quickly. Here are some to think about asking a foreclosing lender:

1. **Will you, the lender, do a short sale?**
   Almost certainly in today's climate the answer will be a conditional yes. The conditions will be spelled out as you proceed.
2. **Do you need an authorization letter to speak to my agent, lawyer, title company, and so forth?**
   Again, the answer will almost certainly be, yes. They may have a form they prefer which they will fax to you. See the example later in this chapter.
3. **Will I need to have a buyer in hand before you'll consider the short sale? Or will you make a precommitment?**
   Today, beyond saying they will want to look at your hardship, most lenders will definitely want a buyer in hand, including a purchase agreement.

4. **Do you want a short sale packet of documents? What should go into it?**

   Almost certainly they will. Many lenders will fax you a sheet of paper explaining what goes into the package. (See Chapter 8).

5. **Where do I begin?**

   The usual answer is the authorization letter, followed by the short sale package.

6. **How long will it take you to act, once you get all the documents you need?**

   Answers such as "As quickly as possible" or "Soon" are not going to be helpful. Answers such as "Within 3 days" are.

7. **To whose attention should I send documents? What is the correct current fax number or address?**

   Unfortunately, the numbers and addresses seem to change all the time, almost as quickly as staff changes. Once you get a name, address, and a number, try to use them as soon as you can.

What you accomplish when you contact the loss mitigation department of a foreclosing lender is to find someone to talk to—find the right party to send documents to. And you get the fax number or address where to send them. *Note:* Some lenders will only look at packets sent physically through the mail or by messenger. Others will only look at faxes—probably the majority.

When You Have an Agent

The agent should apprise you of all this, but almost immediately he or she will want you to send an authorization letter to the lender. That allows the lender to talk about your finances to the agent as well as a whole host of others who may become involved in the short sale. Figure 6.1 illustrates a sample authorization letter.

TIP

The authorization letter typically lists the name of those people, such as your real estate agent, who will be contacting the lender. It might also include a number of "John Does" just in case there's someone else in their offices who needs to speak to the lender about you. To protect your privacy, you may want to restrict the letter of authorization to only a few named individuals, such as Peter Smith and Jane Miller of ZYX Realty only or Mike Gonzales, attorney.

Be Careful to Whom You Give Permission

The information that you authorize your lender to give out tends to be highly confidential in nature. It might include things such as your name, age, place of birth, date of birth, social security number, credit score and report, bank account info, and so on. Unless you are willing to have this information shared, *do not* send a letter of authorization.

Most people normally do not want to share this kind of information. However, when trying to avoid foreclosure with a short sale being an alternative, they often don't care. If you're not sure, check with an attorney to see what the consequences of sending a letter of authorization will be for you.

TRAP

If someone else such as an agent or a buyer prepares the authorization letter for you, read it carefully and be sure you understand its terms. Some letters give out your power of attorney. That could mean that your home could be sold without your knowledge or permission. You probably don't want this. Be sure to check with your attorney.

Dealing with the FHA

If your foreclosing mortgage is insured by the FHA (Federal Housing Administration), you have a special situation to deal with.

Letter of Authorization

Date:

Property and Mortgage/Lien Holder Information
Property and borrower/homeowner information

Property address: _____City: _____ State: _____

Property owner(s) name:_____ and _____

Primary borrower SSN:_____ Coborrower SSN: _____

To: First mortgage/lien holder: _____
Re: First mortgage or loan/account number:_____

To: Second mortgage/lien holder:_____
Re: Second mortgage or loan/account number: _____

To: Other mortgage/lien holder: _____
Re: Other mortgage or loan/account number: _____

To Whom It May Concern:

I, _____, and _____,
             Borrower   Coborrower

herewith give the above referenced mortgage holder/lender, attorney, servicer, and/or insurer of the mortgage loan or credit card debt referenced above permission to speak with and disclose financial records pertaining to the loan or debt to John Smith of Smith Associates, Friendly Title Company, ABCD Realty, and/or each of their respective assigns, associates, employees, or agents.

A facsimile copy of this document may serve with all the rights and legalities as an original.

Accordingly, I agree to indemnify and hold harmless John Smith of Smith Associates, Friendly Title Company, ABCD Realty and/or each of their respective assigns, associates, employees, or agents from any liability for actions taken by the lender or as a result of this contemplated short sale transaction.

Dated this, the ____ day of July, 2009.

_____   _____
Borrower   Coborrower

Figure 6.1 Authorization letter: A sample letter signed by the seller that authorizes the lender to speak with designated people such as the seller's attorney and/or agent. Check with your attorney before signing any authorization letter.
Download at www.realestateradiousa.com/freedocuments/
letter_of_authorization.doc.

The U.S. Department of Housing and Urban Development (HUD) has a preforeclosure sale program (PFS) designed with a loss mitigation process for families facing foreclosure.

It demands that the borrower follow a very specific procedure that is different from that of other lenders. It involves getting an FHA appraisal of the current value of the property, limits the buyer's closing costs (it will pay to 1 percent, providing the buyer obtains new FHA financing), and restricts the amount of the appraised value of the property that the FHA will accept to between 84 and 88 percent, depending on how long it takes to market the home. Of special interest is that the FHA will allow the seller to get a check for $1,000 on closing!

There are other terms and conditions. For example, the FHA will allow the discharge of junior leans—second, third, and so on mortgages—up to $2,500. And you cannot list the house for less than the FHA-appraised value.

One problem with the FHA PFS program is that its terms tend to change frequently. If you are interested in it, I suggest you check it out online. A good place to start is with a mortgage letter recently issued. As of this writing, this letter of instruction can be found at: www.hud.gov/offices/adm/hudclips/letters/mortgagee/files/08-43ml.doc.

If the Web address changes, check into www.hud.gov.

Lenders' Loss Mitigation Phone List

Following is a list of phone numbers for lenders (either directly to their loss mitigation number or for their offices). There are over 8,000 lenders across the country; this is a group of some of the majors. Please note that these numbers will change over time. To find the loss mitigation committee or officer for your particular lender, you may need to begin at a local office and make calls working your way up.

American Home Mortgage
Schaumberg, IL
877-304-3100

American Home Mortgage Servicing
Loss Mitigation
888-275-2648

Amtrust Bank
888-696-4444

Aurora Loan Services Home Retention Dept.
800-550-0508

Austin Bank
Longview, TX
888-758-2265

Avelo Mortgage
LLC Home Retention Dept.
866-992-8356

BankNorth
Portland, ME
800-462-3666

Bank of America
Home Retention Dept.
800-846-2222

Bank of Hawaii
Honolulu, HA
888-643-3888

Carrington Mortgage Services
Home Retention Dept.
800-790-9502

Mitigation

2, ext. 52195

...annattan Mortgage

800-446-8939

Ohio Servicing Center: 800-526-0072

Florida Servicing Center: 800-527-3040

Chevy Chase Bank

800-933-9100

Citi Mortgage

Loss Mitigation

888-219-1433

City Residential Lending

800-211-6926

Colonial Savings

Fort Worth, TX

800-937-6002

Countrywide Home Loans

Thousand Oaks, CA

800-669-6607

Ditech

800-852-0656

Downey S&L

Newport Beach, CA

800-824-6902

EMC Mortgage Corporation

Loss Mitigation

800-723-3004

Fifth Third Bank
Loss Mitigation
800-375-1745

First Franklin Loan Services
Home Loan Services/NationPoint Loan Services Loss Mitigation
800-622-5035

First Horizon Bank
Loss Mitigation, First Mortgage
800-707-9998
Loss Mitigation, Second Mortgage
800-396-6784

Fremont Investment & Loan
866-484-0291

GMAC ResCAp
GMAC Mortgage, Homecomings Financial, GMAC Bank
Default Division
800-799-9250

Home Loan Services, Inc. Servicer for First Franklin Loan Services, NationPoint Loan Services, and National City Bank
Loss Mitigation
800-622-5035

HomEq
Home Retention Dept.
877-867-7378

HSBC North America Household Finance
800-338-4626

Huntington Bank
800-290-3359

Huntington Mortgage Group
Home Retention Dept.
800-323-9865

IndyMac Bank
Loss Mitigation
877-736-5556

Iowa Bankers Mort. Corp.
800-532-1423

JPMorgan Chase
Loss Mitigation
800-446-8939

Litton Loan Servicing
Loss Mitigation
800-548-8665

M & I Bank
Greenwood, IN
866-473-4333

Midland Mortgage
800-552-3000

National City Mortgage
Loss Mitigation
800-622-5035

NationPoint Loan Services
Loss Mitigation
800-622-5035

Nation Star Mortgage
Loss Mitigation
888-850-9398

North American Savings
Grandview, MO
800-677-6272

Ocwen Federal Bank
800-746-2936

Ocwen Loan Servicing
LLC Loss Mitigation
877-596-8580

Popular Service Mortgage
Debt Collection
866-361-3460

Prodovis Mortgage
LLC Home Retention Dept.
888-878-0522

Saxon Mortgage Services, Inc.
Delinquent: 888-325-3502
Not Delinquent: 800-594-8422

Select Portfolio Servicing Loss Mitigation
888-349-8968

SunTrust Mortgage, Inc.
Loss Mitigation
800-443-1032

Third Federal Savings
888-844-7333

US Bank
800-365-7900

Wachovia (see Wells Fargo)

Washington Mutual Bank

Loss Mitigation Prime: 866-926-8937

Loss Mitigation Subprime: 888-708-4696

Washington Mutual (see JP Morgan Chase)

Wells Fargo Home Mortgage

Loss Mitigation: 888-231-0757

Wells Fargo Financial Loss Mitigation

800-275-9254

Wilshire Credit Corporation

Loss Mitigation

888-917-1050; 888-502-0100

Why Not Try a
Loan Modification?

My wife recently asked me a question I had never put into words, but which was very logical. "If lenders are willing to do a short sale for a seller, why aren't they willing to give that seller a loan discount of the same amount so he or she can keep the property?" In other words, if the lender is willing to cut the loan amount by 30 percent so the seller can sell, why wouldn't it cut the loan amount by 30 percent so the seller could end up with lower payments and stay in the home?

The benefits of doing this should be obvious. A great many troubled sellers/borrowers, perhaps more than half, could remain in their homes and avoid the disruptions that a forced move entails. It would also greatly reduce the number of foreclosures. And it might stabilize property values in areas where they are falling and even help end a recession. It's one of those ideas that on the surface has only plusses.

Yet when a borrower comes to a lender's loan modification committee (as opposed to a loss mitigation committee which handles short sales and sometimes foreclosures), a reduction of the mortgage amount seems to always be the last thing on the table. Yes, payments can be delayed or in some cases forgiven. The loan term can be extended out to 40 years. Sometimes even a slight reduction in the interest rate can be obtained. But only grudgingly will a loan modification committee consider reducing the amount of a loan, and only then when the Obama housing incentive plan is invoked. For more on "The Obama Housing Plan," see below.

TRAP

Sometimes when you as a borrower seek a loan modification, you're not really speaking to the people who have the power to make a serious change to your mortgage. Rather, your "lender" is actually nothing more than a servicer for a silent partner, a secondary lender whom you may never see or talk to. The silent partner calls the shots and may determine just what sort of modifications are going to be allowed.

Why?

It was so good a question that I attempted to put it to several major lenders. I called Bank of America, Chase, Citi, and Wells Fargo. I never got through to anyone who could give me a good answer. Although I did call one smaller lender, a representative of which talked to me on condition of anonymity. He said that the reason was fear of the "cascade effect."

What on earth is the cascade effect?

It works like this. When people come before a loan modification committee, generally they are behind in their payments but are not always in foreclosure. Hopefully, they should have a variety of alternatives. One good solution would be to refinance their loan with an outside lender to a lower interest rate, even to an ARM with a new three-year low teaser rate and much lower payments.

They can't do this, however, because usually they are under water; they owe more than their collateral—their house—is worth. No outside lender will give them a new mortgage.

Further, if they are behind on their mortgage payments (and likely behind on other payments as well), their credit probably can't handle a new mortgage. Hence, the best alternative isn't available.

> **TIP**
>
> The most common kind of loan modifications are *forbearances*, where you are allowed to forgo making payments for a few months but then are expected to later catch up, and a *repayment plan*, which is a guideline for making up lost payments over time. A reduction of the actual loan amount is almost never in the cards. Nor is a long-term reduction of the interest rate, although a temporary reduction may be possible.

Why, then, doesn't the existing lender simply reduce the loan amount to the current market value of the home? If this were done, the lower loan balance would greatly reduce the monthly payments. It could save the borrower from having to attempt a short sale and could prevent foreclosure.

As I said, "Why not?"

The reason apparently is that many lenders fear a cascade of demands for this kind of mortgage modification. If they grant a loan balance reduction for one under-water borrower, they fear that tomorrow 10 more will be asking and the next day 100 more. Remember, more than 90 percent of mortgage borrowers, including those who are under water, are still making payments on their loans. However, in a cascade effect the fear is that very soon *everyone* who has a mortgage and is under water (even those not behind in their payments) will want their lender to reduce the mortgage amount. (In this way the homeowners could throw a sizeable portion of their home's lost value onto the lender.) The loss to the lender would be catastrophic and would quickly eat up its capital. It could soon become insolvent, even with government bailouts.

TRAP

More than half of the 287,755 mortgage workouts in the third quarter of 2008 involved repayment plans that actually *increased* the monthly payments, mainly to make up for past missed payments. As a result more than half of borrowers who had loan modifications redefaulted within six months. (Office of Controller of the Currency.)

Therefore, lenders tend to stick by their guns and generally refuse to modify mortgages downward. They see it as self-preservation. For borrowers, however, it's often catastrophic and forces them into a short sale to avoid foreclosure.

Cram Downs

In the trade a "cram down" is when a lender is *forced* to modify a mortgage by lowering the amount owed, whether it wants to or not. It's like the discount is being "crammed down its throat"!

Understandably most lenders do not like cram downs. However, they used to face them regularly as part of bankruptcy proceedings. Prior to 1978, bankruptcy judges had the authority to force a lender to modify the loan amount and terms as part of the bankruptcy settlement. When the borrower took it to the judge, the judge could cram down a mortgage discount on the lender as well as reduce the interest rate and other terms of the loan.

However, in 1978 that authority was reduced to just cram downs and not reduction in interest rates or extension of the terms of the loan. Then in a court case in 1993 (*Nobelman v. American Savings Bank*) the Supreme Court held that crams down were likewise prohibited.

This applies to Chapter 13 bankruptcy where debts are generally restructured to allow the debtor to pay them off over time. (Chapter 7 bankruptcy involves disposing of a debtor's assets to pay off creditors and may not be available to individuals.)

There is, however, a strong movement afoot as of this writing to once again allow bankruptcy judges to have the power to cram down mortgages on lenders. It has been opposed, however, by most (but not all) bankers. As of this writing, its chances for passage seem mixed. (But who knows? Check with an attorney to see what the status is when you read this.)

The advantage for the borrower if bankruptcy judges were to have the power to force crams downs can be enormous. If you're in serious financial straits and are seeking bankruptcy, the judge could then reduce the amount you owe (and the amount of your payments), and you might be able to save your house.

Of course, going into bankruptcy just to save your house probably doesn't make sense for most people. A bankruptcy is carried on your credit report almost as long as a foreclosure. It's like cutting off your nose to spite your face.

On the other hand, the *threat* of going into bankruptcy, if the judge could actually force cram downs, could make a huge difference. If you went into a loan modification meeting and said that your choices were either getting your loan modified downward or going into bankruptcy where the judge might order it, the lenders would probably pay a whole lot more attention. And more significant loan modifications might happen.

Of course, in many cases, if not most, simply getting the loan amount reduced may not save the property for the borrower who is in serious financial distress, and a short sale may still be needed. This is especially the case when there's job loss, divorce, illness, or even a loan that, when reduced, is still too big for the borrower to handle.

However, if cram downs were permitted, when trying to get a lender to approve a short sale, including the threat of the borrower going into bankruptcy in the hardship letter could very well make the lender more amenable to accepting the sale.

TRAP

Never consider bankruptcy without first consulting with your financial advisor and a good lawyer. It's a very big step to take, with financial ramifications that could last for years.

As noted, check with your financial advisor, or a good attorney, to see if Congress has changed the law with regard to cram downs at the time you read this.

FHASecure Program

The FHASecure program is for creditworthy homeowners who have missed payments when their loans reset to higher interest rates. It is aimed primarily at subprime borrowers as well as those with adjustable rate mortgages that reset. Begun in 2007, it was expanded in 2008 to include

> Borrowers with adjustable rate mortgages who were late on two consecutive monthly mortgage payments or at two different times over the previous 12 months. FHA will require a 97 percent loan-to-value (LTV) ratio for these borrowers to refinance, the same LTV as FHA's current standard.
>
> Borrowers with adjustable rate mortgages who were late on three consecutive monthly mortgage payments or at three different times over the past 12 months. FHA will require a 90 percent LTV ratio for these borrowers to refinance.

Under this program, it's up to lenders to voluntarily write down the mortgage value to a principal balance of 90 to 97 percent LTV (loan-to-[current] value). (No cram downs—the FHA insures mortgages to lenders who make them; it rarely loans money directly to borrowers.) The FHA also encourages secondary financing to fill the gap between the new mortgage and current market values.

Of course, to participate, a borrower must meet the FHA's strict creditworthiness standards, a big drawback if you're having

financial troubles. And there's an insurance premium that
paid to the FHA.

For more information on this program, check into:
www.hud.gov/news/release.cfm?content=pr08-050.cfm.

If this Web address is not available, go to www.hud.gov and use
keyword FHASecure to find the current location for information
on the program.

The Obama Housing Plan

As this book went to press, the Obama administration announced
a housing plan that could help some people who are under water
and who cannot make their payments. (It apparently will do little
for those can afford to make their payments and are deeply under
water.)

Under the new program, if you're under water and have higher
payments than you can afford, your lender will be given an incentive to modify your mortgage. (The incentive would be in the
form of cash for $1,000 or more—to your lender.)

The modification would be to reduce your payments to a maximum of 38 percent of your income. (Currently, many households
are paying 50 percent or more of their income in monthly payments—generally speaking an unsustainable amount.)

Furthermore, the government would then use its own money
to further reduce your payments to 31 percent of your income.
This is considered sustainable by most mortgage lenders. The
reduction would be accomplished by extending the term of the
mortgage, reducing the interest rate, or, as a last resort, reducing
the principal.

For example, your payments are $2,000 a month, and your
income is $4,000. You're at 50 percent. Under the program, your
payments might be reduced to $1,240 a month. The hope is that,

at the lower amount, you would be able to make your payments and keep your home.

The terms of the program include the following:

- You must be under water and not be able to afford your monthly payments.
- You must apply within three years of the program start.
- Investors need not apply; it's only for owner-occupants.
- The mortgage payment reduction is good for five years.
- It's up to the lender's discretion whether or not to put you into the program. If the lender makes a judgment call that it can save more money by proceeding with foreclosure, it can refuse to modify your mortgage.

If you still have equity but less than the 20 percent now required in most cases to refinance, you would be able to refi. Further, the refi would be without the need for PMI (private mortgage insurance—now required on refis of greater than 80 percent LTV—loan-to-value). You could refinance through Freddie Mac or Fannie Mae provided your home isn't more than 5 percent under water. The new loan would be for a low interest rate, presumably for 30 years and fully amortized (no interest-only loans).

Details of the Obama plan will be finalized and the plan itself implemented over three years. To find out if you might qualify, check with a good mortgage broker. Also check out www.financialstability.gov, which presents explanations of many government bailout programs.

Loan Modification Fixes

Be wary of people who tell you that they can modify your loan for you, especially if a fee is involved, especially if that fee is up front. Generally others can only do what you can do for yourself.

A lot of scams have been making the rounds where a seemingly credible company or individual seeks money, usually up front, to modify the payments of your loan. All too often nothing happens with your loan, and the fixer simply disappears with your money.

This is not to say that you shouldn't consult a good attorney or mortgage broker for advice and help on getting your mortgage modified. These people can provide help, and they may reasonably want to charge for it. But usually, they will not simply say something like, "Pay me and forget it. I'll do it all for you." Typically to get a modification you personally will want to appear or present documents before the lender's loan modification committee and present your own case, although you may be able to have experts, such as an attorney, help you.

Don't throw good money after bad by getting stung in a loan scam. (See also Chapter 13.)

At a Loan Modification Meeting

If you attend a loan modification meeting, here's what the lender is likely to do:

- Forgive missed back payments.
- Forgive assessed penalties and back interest.
- Extend the term of the loan out to 40 years to help reduce monthly payments.
- Reduce slightly the interest rate (if the existing interest rate on the mortgage happens to be higher than the current market interest rate).
- Offer to counsel you on money management, including handling your other bills.
- Try to come up with a payment you can afford.

Here's what the lender is *not* likely to do:

- Reduce the amount of your mortgage.
- Significantly reduce the interest rate on your loan or significantly reduce your monthly payment.

Putting Together the Short Sale Package

The short sale package is the key to the door that opens the lender's heart.

This sounds sentimental, but in effect that's what it does. (Of course, it could be argued that there is no door because lenders have no heart! But that's just refusing to admit that, for them, it has to be all business and not be personal.)

The package should contain all the information that your lender needs to make a decision about whether to allow a short sale on your property. You should have previously contacted the lender to see exactly what is required. (See Chapter 6.) And now you should accumulate all the necessary documents.

Once you have the package assembled, you or your agent can send it in by mail, although I suggest expedited delivery such as FedEx or UPS. Some lenders, of course, prefer that it all come in on a fax machine.

TIP

If you're using an agent, show him or her this chapter to help him or her assemble a complete package to send.

You don't usually want to send in incomplete packages (unless instructed to do so by the lender). The reason is that it tends to hold things up. A checker will quickly discover what's missing, and your package could end up sitting in a basket until the needed documents arrive. Then there's the hassle of finding your package and putting the documents in. And then the whole thing may go to the bottom of the pile again.

Below is a list of what a typical short sale package will contain. You may need fewer items, or more. Below the list is a brief explanation of the various items and where you can usually obtain them:

TIP

You should show your short sale package both to the foreclosing lender as well as to any other junior mortgage holders. Some foreclosing lenders won't consider a short sale until they have releases from junior lenders. (See Chapter 2.)

Here's what your short sale package should contain:

- Proposal offer to lender.
- Lender's net sheet or estimated HUD-1.
- Authorization to release information (if it has not already been sent; see Chapter 6).
- Purchase contract signed by buyer.
- Seller's financial information (the lender may have its own form it wants you to use). This should include supporting financial information (two years of W-2s or 1040s, if self-employed, three months of the most recent pay stubs, and three months of the most recent bank statements.)
- Seller's hardship letter. This should include supporting information such as

 - Medical bills.
 - Disability statements.
 - Unemployment check stubs.
 - Liens on the property.
- Appraisal of the property. This should include the broker's price opinion (BPO) or your own comps (comparable properties) of three current comparable homes for sale and three that sold recently.
- Estimate of any repairs, including supporting information such as estimates from contractors.
- Payoffs on other mortgage or liens on the property.

The Package Proposal Offer to Lender

The proposal offer to the lender typically takes the place of a cover letter. It gives a brief description of the deal and often will tell the lender what its net is going to be. You'll also want to include a "net sheet" or HUD-1 estimate (see below).

The proposal offer to the lender is important. It makes sense of the overall package. Without it you've just got a jumble of documents that a lender may or may not make sense of.

You can write up the proposal offer yourself, or you can have your agent do it. A typed letter is fine; it does not need to be handwritten. See Figure 8.1 for a sample proposal offer to a lender.

The letter shown in the figure can be found at http://www.realestateradiousa.com/freedocuments/offer_and_proposal_letter.doc/, where it may be downloaded.

Lender's Net Sheet or HUD-1

A HUD-1 is a document prescribed by HUD under RESPA (Real Estate Settlement Procedures Act) that must be given to all parties

Date:

To: Loss Mitigation Representative
Lender: MORTGAGES-R-US
Borrower: Fred Smith
Property Address: 123 Town Lane, Anywhere, FL 33333
Reference Loan Number: 123456789

NET AMOUNT OF SHORT SALE OFFER TO MORTGAGES-R-US $200,000.00

Dear Loss Mit Rep:

We are submitting for your review and subsequent approval, this comprehensive **SHORT SALE SUMMARY PACKAGE** pursuant to our recent telephone conversation regarding the possibility of a discounted payoff on the aforementioned defaulted mortgage loan.

We are working very closely with your Borrower to facilitate a sale of the above referenced property. We have in fact entered into a purchase and sale contract (attached). I represent the buyers and my clients are seeking to buy the property without the need for a mortgage contingency and subject only to your approval of this short sale proposal. Inspections have been completed. This sale requires and is contingent upon your approval of the short sale offer

Subsequent to our short sale package being approved by a foreclosing lender, we can close very quickly. We guarantee a closing of the transaction within 5–10 days of acceptance of our offer.

We have been given complete authorization by the Borrower to discuss the mortgage loan that is presently in default that you are seeking to foreclose. We have again included a signed Letter of Authorization executed by the Borrower, which has been previously faxed to you

Our offer is $225,000.00 which will net your bank **$200,000.00** after all closing costs and expenses which you can see on the Estimated HUD Statement attached hereto.

We understand that in order for our offer to be accepted that there may be additional due diligence which may need to be completed. Should a second Broker's Price Opinion (BPO) be necessary, or if one has never been completed, we urge you to have one completed and as we have control of the property we would like to meet with your representative to ensure a proper assessment of the scope of repairs of the subject property and a true and accurate appraisal of the estimated "AS-IS" value of the subject property.

In order to obtain the most accurate valuation, it is our belief that it is imperative that the interior of the house be viewed and that the BPO not be limited to a cursory drive-by viewing or desktop appraisal or automated valuation. We can provide interior access to the house to your representative and will meet with your representative with 48 hours notice.

As an auction date is pending in the very near future, we believe TIME IS OF THE ESSENCE in resolving this matter. We are prepared to close this transaction within 5-10 business days from receiving written notification of your acceptance of this offer or our acceptance of any counter offer that you may make in response to our offer.

If you have any questions, please do not hesitate to contact us as necessary as we stand ready to facilitate and expedite a short sale payoff on the aforementioned loan.

Sincerely,
Your Name
Name of Real Estate Office
Address
City, State Zip Code
Direct Phone:
Direct Fax:
Email:

Figure 8.1 Proposal offer. Courtesy of RealEstateRadioUSA.com

at least one day before a sale closes. Lenders will prepare it as part of the transaction (see Figure 8.2 for a sample). However, some lenders may require that you fill out an *estimated* HUD-1 as part of your short sale package. The advantage is that it shows all the costs of the transaction. From the sheet the lender can see what costs it's going to be liable for.

If no HUD-1 is required (and even if it is), it's usually advisable to include a lender's net sheet. This shows the lender a comparison between what it will net from a short sale and what it will net if it continues with a foreclosure. It is especially useful in demonstrating to the lender that it can save money by doing a short sale. See Figure 8.3 for a sample.

You or your agent will need to create the net sheet. It's important that you be as accurate as possible on all your figures. Find out if lien holders will sign releases, or if they want a payoff of some sort. (See Chapter 2.) Most information can be obtained from a title company, contractors (see below), or your bank.

Purchase Contract Signed by Buyer

As of this writing, most lenders will not consider a short sale until you have a buyer ready to go. This means that you need to first find a buyer and then include the buyer's purchase offer.

Typically the buyer will have an agent who presents the offer to your agent (or directly to you, if you're selling on your own). Since you're basically getting no cash out of the deal, before you sign you should be sure that the contract is likely to be acceptable to the lender so that you will be able to go forward with a short sale. This usually means that the price should be close to market and that there be no excessive costs or unusual demands. Also be sure it contains clauses that allow you to back out of the deal without liability if the lender will not accept it (see below).

A. Settlement Statement

U.S. Department of Housing
and Urban Development

OMB Approval No. 2502-0265

B. Type of Loan

1. ☐ FHA 2. ☐ FmHA 3. ☐ Conv. Unins. 4. ☐ VA 5. ☐ Conv. Ins.	6. File Number:	7. Loan Number:

8. Mortgage Insurance Case Number:

C. Note: This form is furnished to give you a statement of actual settlement costs. Amounts paid to and by the settlement agent are shown. Items marked "(p.o.c.)" were paid outside the closing; they are shown here for informational purposes and are not included in the totals.

D. Name & Address of Borrower:	E. Name & Address of Seller:	F. Name & Address of Lender:

G. Property Location:	H. Settlement Agent:	
	Place of Settlement:	I. Settlement Date:

J. Summary of Borrower's Transaction		K. Summary of Seller's Transaction	
100. Gross Amount Due From Borrower		**400. Gross Amount Due To Seller**	
101. Contract sales price		401. Contract sales price	
102. Personal property		402. Personal property	
103. Settlement charges to borrower (line 1400)		403.	
104.		404.	
105.		405.	
Adjustments for items paid by seller in advance		Adjustments for items paid by seller in advance	
106. City/town taxes to		406. City/town taxes to	
107. County taxes to		407. County taxes to	
108. Assessments to		408. Assessments to	
109.		409.	
110.		410.	
111.		411.	
112.		412.	
120. Gross Amount Due From Borrower		**420. Gross Amount Due To Seller**	
200. Amounts Paid By Or In Behalf Of Borrower		**500. Reductions In Amount Due To Seller**	
201. Deposit or earnest money		501. Excess deposit (see instructions)	
202. Principal amount of new loan(s)		502. Settlement charges to seller (line 1400)	
203. Existing loan(s) taken subject to		503. Existing loan(s) taken subject to	
204.		504. Payoff of first mortgage loan	
205.		505. Payoff of second mortgage loan	
206.		506.	
207.		507.	
208.		508.	
209.		509.	
Adjustments for items unpaid by seller		Adjustments for items unpaid by seller	
210. City/town taxes to		510. City/town taxes to	
211. County taxes to		511. County taxes to	
212. Assessments to		512. Assessments to	
213.		513.	
214.		514.	
215.		515.	
216.		516.	
217.		517.	
218.		518.	
219.		519.	
220. Total Paid By/For Borrower		**520. Total Reduction Amount Due Seller**	
300. Cash At Settlement From/To Borrower		**600. Cash At Settlement To/From Seller**	
301. Gross amount due from borrower (line 120)		601. Gross amount due to seller (line 420)	
302. Less amounts paid by/for borrower (line 220)	( )	602. Less reductions in amt. due seller (line 520)	( )
303. Cash ☐ From ☐ To Borrower		**603. Cash** ☐ To ☐ From Seller	

Section 5 of the Real Estate Settlement Procedures Act (RESPA) requires the following: • HUD must develop a Special Information Booklet to help persons borrowing money to finance the purchase of residential real estate to better understand the nature and costs of real estate settlement services; • Each lender must provide the booklet to all applicants from whom it receives or for whom it prepares a written application to borrow money to finance the purchase of residential real estate; • Lenders must prepare and distribute with the Booklet a Good Faith Estimate of the settlement costs that the borrower is likely to incur in connection with the settlement. These disclosures are mandatory.

Section 4(a) of RESPA mandates that HUD develop and prescribe this standard form to be used at the time of loan settlement to provide full disclosure of all charges imposed upon the borrower and seller. These are third party disclosures that are designed to provide the borrower with pertinent information during the settlement process in order to be a better shopper.

The Public Reporting Burden for this collection of information is estimated to average one hour per response, including the time for reviewing instructions, searching existing data sources, gathering and maintaining the data needed, and completing and reviewing the collection of information.

This agency may not collect this information, and you are not required to complete this form, unless it displays a currently valid OMB control number.

The information requested does not lend itself to confidentiality.

Figure 8.2 The closing statement required under RESPA (Real Estate Settlement Procedures Act) which shows all the costs of the sale including closing costs.

L. Settlement Charges

700. Total Sales/Broker's Commission based on price $ @ % =	Paid From Borrowers Funds at Settlement	Paid From Seller's Funds at Settlement
Division of Commission (line 700) as follows:		
701. $ to		
702. $ to		
703. Commission paid at Settlement		
704.		
800. Items Payable In Connection With Loan		
801. Loan Origination Fee %		
802. Loan Discount %		
803. Appraisal Fee to		
804. Credit Report to		
805. Lender's Inspection Fee		
806. Mortgage Insurance Application Fee to		
807. Assumption Fee		
808.		
809.		
810.		
811.		
900. Items Required By Lender To Be Paid In Advance		
901. Interest from to @$ /day		
902. Mortgage Insurance Premium for months to		
903. Hazard Insurance Premium for years to		
904. years to		
905.		
1000. Reserves Deposited With Lender		
1001. Hazard insurance months@$ per month		
1002. Mortgage insurance months@$ per month		
1003. City property taxes months@$ per month		
1004. County property taxes months@$ per month		
1005. Annual assessments months@$ per month		
1006. months@$ per month		
1007. months@$ per month		
1008. months@$ per month		
1100. Title Charges		
1101. Settlement or closing fee to		
1102. Abstract or title search to		
1103. Title examination to		
1104. Title insurance binder to		
1105. Document preparation to		
1106. Notary fees to		
1107. Attorney's fees to		
(includes above items numbers:)		
1108. Title insurance to		
(includes above items numbers:)		
1109. Lender's coverage $		
1110. Owner's coverage $		
1111.		
1112.		
1113.		
1200. Government Recording and Transfer Charges		
1201. Recording fees: Deed $; Mortgage $; Releases $		
1202. City/county tax/stamps: Deed $; Mortgage $		
1203. State tax/stamps: Deed $; Mortgage $		
1204.		
1205.		
1300. Additional Settlement Charges		
1301. Survey to		
1302. Pest inspection to		
1303.		
1304.		
1305.		
1400. Total Settlement Charges (enter on lines 103, Section J and 502, Section K)		

Figure 8.2 The closing statement required under RESPA *(cont.)*

Lender's Short Sale vs. REO Net Sheet

Lender:_____

Loan No. _____

Property Address: _____

Borrower's Name:_____

Monthly Payment: $3,230

Current status

Months past due: 9

Market value of property*: $300,000

Mortgage balance: $400,000

Short sale offer: $300,000

As is, current

SHORT SALE ACCEPTANCE		AS REO	
Short sale offer	$300,000	Anticipated REO price	$280,000
Lost interest	29,000	Lost interest	29,000
		Added lost interest	19,000
Broker fees	15,000	Broker fees	15,000
Closing costs	10,000	Closing costs	10,000
		Foreclosure costs	7,500
		Added insurance	500
		Added taxes	3,000
		Added maintenance	2,500
		Added utilities	1,000
Title costs	3,500	Added title costs	7,000
TOTAL	$242,500	TOTAL	$185,500

Short sale loss (est.) $157,500   REO sale loss (est.) $214,500

Amount saved by lender in a short sale $57,000

Acceptance of the short sale offer will save the lender: $57,000[†]

[†]Time is of the essence and is an additional incentive. A short sale will immediately remove any further liability from the property and will remove it from the lender's books as "non-performing."

Figure 8.3 Lender's net sheet: An Income/Expense sheet that shows the lender how much it will out of a short sale. It is often combined with a net sheet showing the net from a foreclosure and comparing the two.

TRAP

Many short sale sellers include a clause that the property is sold "as is." This means that while the buyer has the opportunity to discover any defects and the seller the responsibility to disclose them, the seller does not warrant the property—will not be responsible for correcting defects.

Special areas to watch out for in these contracts, in addition to price, include

- A clause that says that the sale is contingent on the lender's acceptance and that you are to incur no expenses or liability if the lender does not accept. You don't want to be liable to a buyer when a lender won't cooperate.
- A clause that says that commission is owed to an agent only if enough is netted from the deal to pay it. It is not to come out of your pocket and to be paid only if the deal actually closes. (See Chapter 4.)
- A clause that states you are not responsible for any repairs to the property. Repairs have to come out of the lender's allowance. (See below.)

Have an agent or an attorney add the needed wording to fit the terms you want and the laws of your state.

Seller's Financial Information

You'll probably have to go hunting for your financial information. Begin with your 1040s, the form you use to file your federal income tax. Often the W-2s are attached. If you're self-employed, you'll probably need two years of the entire 1040.

You'll also need to show the stubs from your paychecks for the last several months. Be sure you hang onto these. If they are not available (for example, you have automatic deposit to a bank account), bring your last several months of checking account statements.

You may also need other financial statements such as from savings accounts, stock brokerage accounts, and so forth. Ideally, these will be used to support your claim of financial hardship. If, however, you have high balances in any of them, they may work against you. The lender may feel that you have the wherewithal to keep making your payments and therefore refuse a short sale.

TIP If you've determined to go forward with a short sale, you'll probably need to give all this information to the lender. It will be hard to keep it confidential. The lender may order a three-bureau credit report on you, which would tend to reveal anything you might be concealing.

Seller's Hardship Letter

A hardship letter is addressed to the lender. In it you explain the reasons you are unable to continue making payments on your home and require a short sale. It should be about one page in length and be to the point; it shouldn't ramble. (Lenders don't have time or patience to read lengthy tomes.)

Your explanation(s) should be reasonable. Your letter should be *reasoned,* not emotional. You may feel highly emotional about the whole situation, but here you need to express those emotions as reasons why a lender would give you a short sale.

Figures 8.4, 8.5, and 8.6 illustrate three sample short sale letters. While you may want to use elements from each of them, you should fashion your own letter in your own words to meet your specific circumstances. The letters preferably should be handwritten legibly in your own handwriting.

The sample hardship letters may be downloaded at: http://www.realestateradiousa.com/freedocuments/hardship_letter_1.doc (...letter_2.doc, ...letter_3.doc)

To: Whom It May Concern

I have been asked to write this letter to give you some reasons why I am unable to pay our mortgage. There is a very simple answer. I don't have the money to do so.

After an exhaustive search to regain employment, my wife Jane, who lost her job a couple of months ago, became quite depressed. She has since sought the comfort of her family and has relocated to our home country, Colombia in South America. Unfortunately, I can not afford the payments on the loan and I have to be with my wife. So next week I will be permanently leaving the United States and returning to Colombia as well.

I understand that this letter will help you to decide whether we deserve to be allowed to sell our property in what I am told is a short sale type of transaction. I cannot afford to enter into any type of deferral program or forebearance agreement as our relocation to Colombia is permanent, and neither my wife nor I will be returning.

The cost of living is much cheaper in Colombia, and although we have no savings or assets remaining, our families have agreed to support us while we get back on our feet. We do not have this kind of support group here.

For months now I have struggled and tried to find a way to sell my house or come up with the money to catch up on my payments, but I have not been able to find any real way to do so. I have listed the home for sale and rent on the MLS since September 2006 but as a result of the sagging real estate market here in South Florida, I have not received a single offer—for rent or sale.

As you can imagine, ever since I began falling behind, I have been getting letters and phone calls from hundreds of people who say that they can help me. Some have wanted money from me, and most were just "investors" who wanted to take my house and leave me out in the cold with some form of scheme or another.

Some have even tried to convince me to file for bankruptcy to fight the foreclosure. Even though it is an option that is available to me, I think it would make matters worse in the long run since I do not have the money to hire an attorney and there would be no way for me to come back and forth from Colombia for court hearings that have no bearing on my future since I do not plan to return to America.

I would prefer to work out a friendly arrangement with your company instead of filing for bankruptcy. I have had one real estate agent approach me who specializes in short sales, and she has a cash buyer available if I can come to some agreement with you.

She has informed me of a way that I may be able to settle this with you and it is by doing a short sale. It has been explained to me and I understand that if you approve it, I can move on with my life and we won't have to go to court and fight over this and I'll never have to file for bankruptcy to fight the foreclosure. I agree that selling the house this way is a much better way to go for all of us.

Financially, I do not have the money to make up the back payments and I would like to avoid anymore hassles. I am embarrassed by this, and sometimes I can't sleep at night worrying about what will happen. It is eating me up inside not being with my wife or being able to pay my mortgage and having to go through this.

(continued on next page)

Figure 8.4 Sample hardship letter to show why the lender should grant a short sale. They should be handwritten, if possible. Courtesy of www.realestateradiousa.com.

I have not been able to make enough money lately to pay my mortgage, and I also have not had the money to keep the house maintained, I don't have any alternative to foreclosure other than doing this short sale.

I still have to wake up every morning as if I were going to work, except now I have to look in the mirror and admit that I have let my family down. I am sorry that I am in this position, but with your help, we can all work this out so that we can avoid a long, drawn out process. Please help me take a big step in getting my feet back on the ground by letting me accept the offer to buy my house in a way that allows them to close the deal by getting a discount from what I owe you.

I don't have anything left that I can sell or pawn, and without enough money to keep the house, I now need to concentrate on helping my family survive.

I don't understand why I have to write this kind of letter because it is really embarrassing. Believe me, if I had my way, I would be making my payments. It would be so much better than watching things go down the tubes.

Hopefully you will approve the deal quickly. I know that you may feel that I do not deserve any favors, but doing this deal also helps your company as well, as I know it is better to do work things out in a friendly way than by going to a bunch of court hearings and costly hassles.

I sincerely hope that this short sale can be done and that we can all move forward and put this matter behind us.

Sincerely,

John Doe

Figure 8.4 Sample hardship letter *(cont.)*

I am writing this letter to explain my current financial situation. About four months ago I was in a horrible car accident. I have had to endure much pain but nothing prepared me for the loss of my job.

Since the loss of my job, I have been unable to maintain a suitable household for my family. My wife became depressed and left with our three kids, Jane, Becky, and John Jr.

I am currently living with friends as I am unable to provide for them much less a mortgage payment.

Also, after the hurricane, I was unable to make repairs to the property. My insurance got cancelled and I was unable to get any assistance and as such our roof leaks and there is a great deal of mold and dry rot.

Times are so unbelievable. This is not the lifestyle that I want for my children. I tried to sell the house on two separate occasions, but I have not received any offers.

I am sorry that I cannot live up to my obligation, but there is nothing else I can do. Can you please consider this short sale request so that I can move on and try to regroup and make sense of my life?

Sincerely,

John Doe

Figure 8.5 Sample hardship letter to show why the lender should grant a short sale. They should be handwritten, if possible. Courtesy of www.realestateradiousa.com.

To Whom It May Concern:

I'm writing today to tell you a little bit about what has happened in my life that has caused me to get into such trouble with my finances and miss payments on my house.

Three years ago when my husband and I bought our home we were only able to qualify for the home loan if we used both of our incomes.

Twelve months ago John was killed in a construction accident, and suddenly I was faced with a mortgage and two kids and only one income which hardly covers the bills.

I have tried for months to sell the house, but where I live, there's a lot of new house construction and condo conversions and my real estate friend says that people would rather pay a little bit more and get new than buy my house that needs some repair.

I work as much as I can at a local grocery store, but my job position pays only $11.00 per hour. My mom and dad help out whenever they can, and they've even loaned me a little money, but they're retired and don't have much to give.

What I would really like to do is sell the house on a short sale so I can get on with my life. I don't want to try and stay in the house until it is foreclosed on and I don't want to go through an eviction after it is auctioned off. The added embarrassment would just be too much.

I do not have any way of making the payments current, and I just can't handle the stress anymore. If you could, I am asking you to accept the short sale offer that Acme Realty is going to give you, as it is the best offer I've had on my house.

Sincerely,

Jane Doe

Figure 8.6 Sample hardship letter to show why the lender should grant a short sale. They should be handwritten, if possible. Courtesy of www.realestateradiousa.com.

Be sure you attach any supporting documents you have to the hardship letters. You can assume that the lender already knows the status of your mortgage—that you've been served a default notice and perhaps have a court date. But it may not know of your other situations. Therefore, you may want to include:

- Copies of your medical bills. If there are simply too many of them, a summary may do, but include the most recent statement from the medical billing offices.
- Statements showing that you are disabled.

- Check stubs from unemployment insurance payments and other similar kinds of documents.
- Liens from other judgments (bad auto loan, medical non-payment, and so on) if these have been placed on the home. (Sometimes, it's easier to include a preliminary title report, which should show all the liens—an agent can help you get this, or you can get it directly from any title insurance company.)

Appraisal Showing Property Value

The short sale often hinges on how much the property is worth in relation to what you owe on it. You need to establish the current market value of your home.

A professional appraisal costs around $300 to $350 and may be unnecessary. Foreclosing lenders don't normally use these themselves in processing a short sale. Rather they rely on a BPO (broker's price opinion). If you're working with an agent, he or she should give you a complimentary BPO. Otherwise, you might need to pay an agent for one. (It usually shows three recent comparable sales and three current comparables for sale.)

The lender, of course, may get its own BPO to confirm what yours says. (The lender usually pays only around $50 to a broker for the service.)

Repair Estimates

The buyer often takes the home "as is" without requiring that any repairs be made to it. Nevertheless, repairs that are needed should be disclosed.

And some repairs which involve health and safety hazards such as black mold, faulty wiring or gas lines, structural damage, and so on may need to be fixed before a sale can proceed. Ideally you will have contacted several contractors who will come in and give you bids. Their estimates should include a description of the damage as well as an itemized cost to repair it. Remember, the costs of any work that needs to be done will typically be subtracted from the lender's net (either in the form of actual work done or in a reduced price to the buyer).

Payoffs

As noted above, if there are secondary liens (seconds, thirds, and so on) or other liens (IRS, property tax, other judgments), you should indicate who the lien holder is and how much the demanded payoff is. While the senior lender whom you are addressing may not allow any payments to these liens, showing them may help establish why you are in such straits and why you need the short sale you propose.

The Bottom Line

The short sale package is the door to the lender's "heart," or at least to its pocketbook. A carefully thought out package with well-written letters and proper documentation is critical to getting a positive response from the lender.

While your agent may help you with putting the package together, it's often going to be up to you to provide the hand-written letters and the documentation (check stubs, medical bills, bank statements, and so on).

I know that it's hard to concentrate on doing this when you're facing the loss of your home. But helping to put a good package together should reap heavy rewards in the future as you get on with your life.

TIP

Decide early on if you want to go through with all of this. Remember, you'll be revealing some very personal financial information. You don't have to do it. But, then again, you probably will not get your short sale if you don't.

Rewards (?) for Missed Payments and Other Tricks

When it comes to convincing a lender to accept a short sale, I'm always reminded of an incident that happened to me many years ago while I was attending college.

I had a car I wanted to get rid of. You can appreciate the situation better if I tell you that my father helped me buy this particular automobile. Without going into brand name and model, I'll just say that it was very plain, even nondescript. It had just enough horsepower to make it up most hills near where I lived, but not enough to "get you into trouble," as my father put it. I, on the other hand, was looking for something a bit sleeker, something that might impress a date.

To help me understand the meaning of a dollar, my father had arranged for the loan on the car to be exclusively in my name, as was the car's title.

Of course, I had a job to make the payments. But there was an advantage here. I could sell the car and buy another any time I wanted. And I desperately wanted to.

I had no equity in the auto (as with most cars, it quickly depreciated) and figured the best way to sell it would be to find a buyer who would just take over the payments. In that way I'd be out from under the loan and could go out and buy a more "suitable" car.

I put an ad in the paper, there was no Craigslist in those days, and soon found a couple who thought the car was ideal for them. I was happy as a clam. I explained to them that they could just take over the loan and pay me nothing, since, as I mentioned, the car had depreciated to the point where I had no equity in it.

I arranged for the couple to meet the lender. The three of us walked into the lender's office and were seated in front of a large desk behind which a man took out a big folder and leafed through it as I carefully explained what we had in mind. He asked the couple a few questions about their credit, and they produced a checkbook to show they had money in the bank and pay stubs to prove he had a good job and could afford the car.

"Hmm," the lender said after thinking for a while. "I don't think so."

I was shocked. "What do you mean?" I asked.

"I don't think we'll transfer the loan. No, I'm sure of it. We won't."

I was flabbergasted, and angry. "But, you must!" I insisted.

"We don't have to," He replied. "You've never missed a payment on your loan. You're a known quantity. A good borrower. Why should we give you up for someone we don't know?"

He closed the file, and we were dismissed.

The couple who wanted to buy the car was embarrassed, as was I. We said something about better luck next time, shook hands, and left. And I still had that old car.

But, not for long.

The next month I didn't make a payment. After 15 days I received a letter notifying me that I had "forgotten" to make my payment and assessing a penalty.

I missed the payment the month after that. This time the letter I received was much more direct and threatened to have the car repossessed and to have my credit ruined.

I figured the time was right. I put another ad in the paper and almost immediately found another couple who also thought the car was right for them. And we marched down to the lender's office once again.

It was the same man with the same folder. He took it out, looked it over, and said, "Hmm."

I explained that the couple wanted to take over the loan and make the payments. They, too, demonstrated that they were able to do it.

"What about the back payments and penalties?" he asked.

I said I'd pay the back interest, since I'd originally agreed to it in the loan. As for the penalties, they'd just have to remain unpaid. The buyer wasn't willing to pay them, and neither was I. The buyer would take up the loan amount where I'd left it off.

The lender's man said the transfer couldn't be made unless all the back penalties were paid.

I said he could have the car back. I said it was pretty much of a wreck anyhow. The buyers winced at that, but they had seen the car and knew it was clean and ran well.

He said, "Hmm. What about your credit? It'll have a repo on it."

I replied, "I'm in college. I don't really care. When I get out I'll get a job and build it back. I'll be fine."

He thought about it a minute more and then said, "Okay. We'll do it."

The paperwork was prepared and signed off while we were there in the office. An hour later I turned over the keys to the happy buyers, and I no longer owned the car or had the loan.

We all shook hands, including the lender, and prepared to leave. And to this day I still remember him waiting until the buyers had left the room and then pulling me aside and saying, "Congratulations on getting out from under!"

I don't know whether he realized I had played him or not.

It all came down to leverage. When I was making the payments, I was very desirable to the lender. It had no reason to want to make any changes or do anything uncomfortable. Why should it transfer the loan? The payments just kept rolling in. I was honest, wanted to preserve my credit, and like a lamb would do just what the lender wanted. I was the ideal borrower. I had no leverage to force the lender to accept a transfer.

However, after I made it clear that I wasn't making any more payments and that the lender would need to repossess the car, things changed. I was no longer a reliable borrower. Indeed, I was the worst kind of borrower possible—the one who would give the car back to the lender and not worry about it. The lender was agreeable, even relieved to get a new borrower on the loan. I had leverage, even though it was of a negative kind, and I was able to force the deal through.

When dealing with lenders, you sometimes need to work hard to make them want to deal with you.

What Should You Do?

Am I suggesting that you purposely miss payments on your home in order to get a short sale?

No, I'm not. Missing payments are reported to credit bureaus and will show up on your credit report and *will* detrimentally affect your credit score. And this could hasten the foreclosure of your home. Of course, they aren't nearly as detrimental as a foreclosure. (Also, remember the story of Jay in Chapter 2 who got a short sale while just being late on his payments a few times.)

However, it's important to understand that the reason lenders normally agree to short sales is hardship on the part of the borrower. Most short sale borrowers admit they would like to continue making payments on their mortgage but *can't*. The mortgage has reset to a higher interest rate and payment, or they're out of work, or they're sick, or they're divorcing, and on and on.

These are hardship reasons. They are spelled out in black and white in a hardship letter (see Chapter 8) that the borrower sends to the lender. They are the leverage that pushes the lender to make an exception to the mortgage agreement and allows a short payoff. The hardship letter "proves" to the lender that it's better off making a short sale than trying to stick with this borrower. (The lender's net sheet "proves" to it that a short sale is better than foreclosing.)

Of course, the lender bases its decision on logical business practices. How much will it lose one way as compared to losing the other? How much more will it cost to refurbish the home and then sell it as a REO (real estate owned) than to take a quick loss as a short sale?

If you haven't missed any payments, there's no *real* threat of having to take the property back through foreclosure, at least not at the moment. Thus the lender is probably reluctant to make a move.

There may be a hypothetical threat. You may *say* you'll let it go. But, it's hard to believe this coming from someone who is right up to date on the payments. You may be the sort (and there are plenty of people like this out there) who will make those monthly payments no matter what. You're an honest, straight-shooting, idealist borrower. The perfect borrower, in fact. So why change anything?

When you unavoidably miss payments on your mortgage, it produces leverage against a difficult lender. It forces the lender to consider that this property is likely to go into foreclosure—that it will have to take it back and deal with it. It forces the lender to weigh the advantages a short sale may offer.

When You're in Good Shape

I was recently playing bridge with some friends, one of whom mentioned a home she had that was under water. She and her husband had bought it a few years earlier as an investment. However, when the real estate market collapsed, it lost value. Now it was worth only half of what she paid, which was nearly $100,000 below what she owed.

"I'd love to get rid of it," she said. "Can I do a short sale?"

"Can't you rent it out?" I asked.

She explained that she did have it rented but that the rental income didn't come close to paying the mortgage payments plus taxes, insurance, and maintenance. "It was okay when the property was going up in value," she said. "But now that it's gone down, what's the future in keeping it rented? I just lose more money every month. It'll take 10 years for it come back up to where I might break even on what I paid. And then there's all the money I'm losing in payments every month."

"So," I said to her, "You have money in the bank. You have another home in which you live. You have good credit. You have a job which provides you with good income. In other words, you can afford to make the monthly payments."

"Of course," she said. "But, I *don't want to*."

The question was, could she do a short sale? She didn't care about getting any money back. She just wanted out.

Will a Lender Do It?

If you were the lender, would you do my friend's short sale?

After all, perhaps a quarter to a third of all homes in the United States are under water. All those have lenders. And if all of the borrowers asked their lenders to reduce their loan amounts to current market value so they could sell their homes, it would cost lenders not millions, not billions, but trillions of dollars. (See the "cascade effect" mentioned in Chapter 7.)

As a result, lenders normally do a short sale only when there's hardship. (And not always even then!)

If you're not a hardship case, you can still try for a short sale. I've heard of one happening once, though never saw it for myself. Or you can wait until you become a hardship case.

Isn't There Any Way I Can Get Some Cash Out of the Deal?

You may have put down cash to purchase the home. You certainly put money into it as part of your monthly payments. But now, when it's time for a short sale, you're told you'll get nothing. Nothing at all!

Isn't there some way to get something out of the sale?

A few (very few) loss mitigation programs provide some payment to the borrower who's, in essence, losing everything. Under the FHA's preforeclosure sale (PFS) program, for example, the seller may receive a check for $1,000 when the deal closes. (See Chapter 6.)

But generally speaking, in most cases the seller gets nothing.

There is one possible exception to this rule, and that's when you have some personal property to sell.

Yes, you're under water. But, at current market price there are several buyers who want to purchase your home. (None, of course, will pay as much as you owe or more, which would net you something out of the sale.)

I've seen homes that have as many as five concurrent offers on a short sale. The buyers really want to purchase the home, but they don't want to overpay for it. Yet, they are still competing with each other.

The competition usually takes the form of offering more cash down and/or a slightly higher price. Of course, that's all designed to impress the lender, not you, the seller. The price never gets high enough to net you something.

You are usually asked to sign the best offer that the lender is likely to accept. Your signature on the purchase agreement is almost perfunctory. Since you presumably don't care, you'll sign anything.

But hold on. What if you're selling personal property as well? For example, what if you have a painting that's worth $5,000. You have to let it go because you're desperate for money. But you think it fits so perfectly in the living room. So you'll sell it for just $3,000 cash, to whomever buys your home on a short sale.

Note that we're dealing with two things here—real property and personal property. The real property is sold by means of the sale agreement. The personal property is sold separately by means of a bill of sale. This is not all that uncommon in real estate transactions.

However, you make it clear that you won't sell your home to any buyer who won't also purchase the painting.

Will that work?

Maybe. You should definitely run it by an attorney and/or your agent who is familiar with the laws in your state. And you should disclose it to the lender. After all, anything that's part of the transaction and *not disclosed* on the HUD-1 form that lists all items at closing could be viewed as fraud against the lender. That's something you definitely want to avoid. (See Chapter 13.)

And there's a question of whether the buyer will actually go through with the purchase of your painting once the escrow closes on your house.

But sometimes an agent can handle it all for you and see that it flies.

Of course, you also have to have a painting that you want to sell. (But, it could just as well be a car, a television, or something else of personal value that you want to dispose of.)

When It's the Buyer's Idea

You're trying to short sale your home. You're still living in it, and a buyer comes by who seems quite interested. That buyer spends some time looking not only at your home but also at your furniture. Then another interested buyer comes by. Then another.

The agent calls and says you've got multiple offers on your home. (As noted, I've seen as many as five concurrent offers on a short sale where the price is low!)

The offers all seem straightforward. They're all for different prices, but are all very close to your asking price. All the buyers seem to have arranged for financing. How do you choose which one to accept?

Then the agent explains the tricky part. One buyer says she also wants to buy some of your furniture, namely two couches and a rug that you have. The buyer is willing to pay you $2,000 cash outside of escrow after the deal closes for the furnishings.

You're not sure you heard right. Those old couches and rug didn't cost $2,000 new, and they're 10 years old. They have spots and burns in them. Why would a buyer want to buy them?

"I think," your agent says, "that what the buyer is really doing is offering you $2,000 in cash to accept her offer." He goes on to explain that she can't really include it in the offer because the HUD-1 statement (which gives all the costs involved in the transaction and on which the lender relies) says that there are no other monies involved in the real estate deal other than what's on the HUD-1 form.

As we've seen, the furniture is not *real estate*. It's *personal* property. Hence it's not included.

"In other words," you say, "The seller is offering me two grand as an outside-of-the-deal incentive to accept her offer."

"Essentially, I think that's it. Unless, she fell in love with your old furniture." your agent replies.

Should You Take the Offer?

Is the buyer's offer legal? Maybe. Check with your attorney to be sure.

Is it ethical? Probably not. After all, if you're swayed by the cash into accepting a *lesser* offer and the lender goes along, then you're essentially cheating the lender out of some money. That's fraud. (On the other hand, if it's the *only* offer you've had, then it's hard to say it's a *lesser* offer.)

Perhaps the buyer is just being charitable. Maybe she really likes your old furniture and thinks it's kitsch. Maybe it's worth two grand to her.

Be careful, however, if the offer is lower than the market value of your home (even if that market value is below what you owe). The buyer may be trying to get you to sign a lowball deal in order to beat out a buyer with a better real estate offer (but no cash for your furniture). Don't be too tempted by the $2,000. Remember that if the deal is too low, the lender won't accept it. And you'll have lost your attempt to salvage your credit (not to mention the two grand which is paid only if the deal goes through).

Keep your eyes on the donut—getting your house sold and saving your credit—not the "maybe" hole of some elusive cash that may never materialize.

Once again, to be safe you should disclose it to the lender. As I said, anything that's part of the transaction and *not disclosed* on the HUD-1 form that lists all items at closing could be construed as fraud against the lender.

Tax Consequences and Other Dangers

I f you're successful in getting a lender to agree to a short sale, the tendency is for you to think, "I'm home free!"

You've got it made—you've gotten out from under the weight of that mortgage—you no longer have to deal with the consequences of owning that house anymore.

Not so fast.

One day many sellers who think that the ordeal is over may get an assessment from the IRS, six months to two years later, telling them that they owe taxes on the amount that the lender forgave. Suddenly, the whole ordeal starts all over again.

Taxed! On the amount the lender forgave. How can it be?

CAUTION

The whole subject of taxation is complex, the rules frequently change, and it's difficult to tell how and if they apply to you. This discussion is intended to give a general overview of how taxation may affect a short sale. However, you should not rely on it. Before entering into a short sale and for all tax advice, seek the services of a tax professional.

The 1099-C

The IRS generally construes the amount forgiven on a mortgage that you legitimately owed as income to you. Your original lender may see it that way, too. And it may issue a 1099-C. This is a federal form that shows income. It goes to the IRS, and a copy is supposed to go to you as well.

However, if you never received it, or, which is more likely, if you got it, saw that it related to that old house and the short sale, and dumped it, you could be in hot water. The IRS, through a document matching program, may have come up with it, matched it to you, and seen that you never reported the "income" or paid taxes on it. The IRS may be assessing you along with back interest and penalties.

This is obviously something you want to avoid if at all possible. If it happens, you want to be on top of it. If you do nothing, the IRS might file a tax lien and take other action.

As it turns out, there may be something you could have done and might still be able to do. (You undoubtedly will need the aid of a good tax professional, if you never took care of the problem when you filed your tax returns and it crops up later.)

Form 982

It turns out that there are some exclusions to the rule that says that you have to pay taxes on the discounted amount of a mortgage after a short sale. The traditional test was whether or not you were insolvent at the time of the short sale. It says that if you were solvent, you owe the tax. If you weren't, you don't.

What is insolvent? It's when you owe more than you have. An example illustrates it best. If you owe $10,000 but only have $2,000, you are generally considered to be insolvent.

If you were in bankruptcy, you are usually considered to be insolvent. If your total debts were in excess of your total assets, you were probably insolvent. There are also special rules with regard to farm expenses, gifts (as when an uncle tells you to forget paying back a loan he gave you on the property), and business expenses.

These can all be addressed on the IRS Form 982—Reduction of Tax Attributes Due to Discharge of Indebtedness. Some tax preparers also like to include a letter explaining how you calculated your assets and debts when claiming you were insolvent.

On the other hand, if you were solvent when you got the mortgage relief, then you could owe tax on the income. That is, except for a recent act of Congress.

The Mortgage Forgiveness Debt Relief Act of 2007

Because of the crisis in home foreclosure and the resulting increase in short sales, in 2007 Congress passed a debt relief act which allows taxpayers to exclude forgiven mortgage debt provided their loan was $2 million or less (for married couples filing jointly; $1 million for married persons filing separately). In other words, although the lender may still send out a 1099-C, you may be able to exclude the income shown on it and thereby avoid paying taxes on it.

Originally the relief act applied only to debt that was forgiven in 2007 to 2009. However, late in 2008 that was extended to 2012.

The rules are fairly straightforward. The debt that was forgiven must have been used to buy, build, or substantially improve the taxpayer's principal residence. The mortgage used to secure that debt must be on that residence (not on, for example, a second home).

If you refinanced the property, the new mortgage is also eligible for the exclusion. But, the amount you can exclude on the refinanced mortgage is limited to the amount (principal) of the original mortgage *at the time of the refi.*

The new rule applies only to mortgage debt on your principal residence. It does not apply to debt that may be forgiven on rental property, business property, second homes, car loans, or credit cards.

The procedure for obtaining this exclusion is that when you receive the 1099-C from the lender showing that the debt is canceled, you then fill out essentially only a few lines on Form 982 and include it when you file your income taxes.

To avoid problems with the IRS, you should check carefully to see that your lender properly filled out the 1099-C. Be especially careful that the lender correctly listed the value of your home (Box 7) and the correct amount for the debt forgiven (Box 2).

When the House Needs Repairs

Unfortunately, while some homes are in great shape, most are not. Most of us have homes that have some deferred maintenance—that need work to bring them up to acceptable shape for selling.

In a traditional sale, where you're getting some equity out of the property, there is typically negotiation that goes on over the work that needs to be done. The buyer gets a professional home inspection that may reveal, for example, that the roof leaks. Then the buyer will usually demand that you fix the roof as a condition of the sale. You fix it, and the cost is subtracted from your equity—from your payoff when the deal closes.

In a short sale, however, that's not the way it's typically handled. Since you're essentially getting nothing out of the sale in the way of cash, you're certainly not going to pay to fix the roof. That means that there are only two other parties who can pay for it. One is the buyer, if he or she purchases the property while knowing about the roof problem and agrees to take care of it. The other is the lender, by lowering the payoff it will accept to accommodate the roof fix.

If a roofer estimates that it will only take a few hundred dollars to take care of it, the buyer may indeed ignore the problem and accept the house as is. If, however, as is sometimes the case, the roofer says it's going to take thousands to fix it, the buyer may refuse to go forward. After all, a house with $10,000 for roof repair is worth considerably less than a house priced at the same market value without a needed roof repair.

Thus, either the roof must be repaired or the price must be lowered (which lowers the lender's payoff).

Since lowering the price may drop the value below market value for the house (based on comparable sales and listings), you must somehow convince the lender to accept a payoff that is below apparent market value.

The way to do this is to include in your package to the lender one or more estimates of the problem as well as the cost of resolving it. (See Chapter 8.) A letter explaining why the problem is reducing the property's value may also help. While the lender can be expected to resist any discount, you can point out that no buyer could reasonably be expected to purchase the property without some resolution of the problem and that even if the lender were to take the property over through foreclosure, it still somehow would have to deal with the problem, probably through a lower price.

It is, of course, up to the lender to accept or reject your argument. This often comes down to the nature of the problem.

Here's a list of home repair problems that can be expected to get the lender's attention and result in a lower payoff:

- **Leaking roof.** If it's a minor leak, it's not going to result in a discounted payoff. But, it probably will if it's serious enough to affect the home's habitability.
- **Cracked foundation—structural damage.** Again, it may come down to habitability. I've seen many homes that do just fine with a cracked foundation; people live in them without problems for years. On the other hand, if the foundation or the structure is in danger of collapse, then corrective work must be done. And the lender will have to discount the mortgage to allow for it, if there's to be a sale one way or another.
- **Black mold.** This is the kiss of death. Nearly all lenders are sensitive to the fact that buyers are deathly afraid of buying a property with black mold in it. It can be a definite deal breaker. On the other hand, correcting black mold can be very expensive. My guess is that if you have a black mold problem and present a couple of estimates from legitimate mold removal companies, most lenders won't hesitate to discount their payoff to accommodate it. Lenders don't want to take back properties with black mold any more than buyers want to purchase them.
- **Safety and habitability issues.** As noted, anything that affects the safety or the habitability of the house is likely to get a lender to go forward with a further discount of the mortgage to pay for it. Otherwise, the house probably can't be sold. On the other hand, items such as recarpeting, painting, and cosmetic repairs are likely to be ignored by a lender.

Check Chapter 5 for hints on preparing the home for sale.

What to Do If You Get a Low BPO

You found a buyer who's ready, willing, and even eager to purchase your home on a short sale. You put together a solid package to present to the lender. It includes your estimate of the property's value showing that, though well below the mortgage principal amount, the home is being sold for a reasonable price based on recent sales for close-to-market price less the cost of needed repairs, agent fees, normal closing costs, and so on. You send it to the lender.

The lender, as part of its standard procedure, now orders its own BPO (broker's price opinion) from an agent with whom it has a business relationship. The agent goes out, looks at the property, and sends in a BPO that's $25,000 higher than your estimate of the property's value. The lender puts a hold on the deal. It lets you know that because you're selling for so much below market, it probably won't go forward. It thinks that perhaps foreclosing will net it more. (See Chapter 8 for an example of a lender's net sheet.)

When this happens, it's time to immediately contact the lender. Talk to anyone you can in the loss mitigation committee. Tell whomever you reach that they have a bad BPO. Ask them to get another. (Lenders sometimes get as many as two or three BPOs for a property—after all, they're paying only about 50 bucks apiece for them.)

Then, get your own BPO. After all, it's just a *broker's price opinion*. Find a broker to give you an opinion that justifies your price. (Your own agent, if you have one, should be willing to do it for nothing, but sometimes paying an outside agent for it demonstrates more credibility.) Be sure that the broker looks at a minimum of three recent sales, including foreclosures, if possible. Also, have the broker look at a minimum of three current property listings. [Sometimes comparable listings (comps) of old sales are harder to find—usually the current listings are very easy to come by.] Then send your BPO to the loss mitigation committee.

If the lender keeps coming up with a higher figure than you do, something is wrong with one of the the BPOs, either yours or the lender's. Remember, the opinion is based on facts—a number of recent comparable resales and current comparable listings. If both brokers use the same comps, the results should be similar. If they are using different comps and come up with widely different results, then perhaps some of the chosen properties aren't really comparable.

Challenge the lender's BPO comps. Maybe they aren't current. Perhaps they're from a different housing tract where prices are higher. Maybe they're for larger homes or homes with bigger lots or pools. Remember, if the comps are similar, the results shouldn't vary much.

Can you really do this?

Sometimes. Some lenders are cooperative. Of course, some are not. They've got thousands of properties to deal with, and if yours becomes the thorn in their side, they might either pay attention to it or ignore it.

Just remember to be polite but insistent. And it won't hurt if your agent knows the ropes and knows the lender.

Beating the Clock

A large part of a successful short sale is understanding the timelines that operate in a foreclosure and beating them. Miss a critical deadline, and no matter how many buyers or how well-intentioned they are, you could lose your property to a foreclosure auction before a short sale can be completed.

TIP Often the biggest single time-frame problem with a short sale is the buyer(s). A buyer may agree to buy and sign a purchase agreement, but in a short sale that agreement needs to be approved by the lender. Sometimes that takes weeks or even months. In the meantime the buyer may have changed her or his mind, or may have found another home to purchase and refuse to move forward with the deal. Too often it just takes too much time. That's why savvy agents and sellers often like to have two or three or more backup buyers waiting in the wings.

The foreclosure process is filled with deadlines. Miss or ignore a deadline at your own peril. No short sale can save a seller who chooses to ignore the foreclosure timeline on his or her property.

What may not always be clear is that as the foreclosure process progresses, the opportunity for the lender to save money on a short sale often diminishes. And along with it goes the lender's incentive to cooperate with you on the short sale. That's why it's important to move on a short sale as early as possible in the foreclosure process and to show the lender that the amount it will receive from the short sale will be more than if it attempts to sell the property on the open market after the foreclosure auction. To make the short sale happen, you must always demonstrate to a lender that it will save money.

Mortgage vs. Trust Deed Timelines

If you're facing foreclosure, it's important to know the timelines that you're up against. A lot of the timeline depends on the kind of mortgage instrument you have, since the procedure for foreclosing is different for each, as are the deadlines.

There are two different types of mortgage instruments used in the United States—the *mortgage* and the *trust deed*. The following covers their different timelines.

TRAP

Since timelines are so important, if you're facing foreclosure, do not rely on just the timelines given on a Web site, or what is suggested here, or even what is given to you by your foreclosing lender. Check with an attorney to see exactly what timeline dates affect you individually.

The Mortgage (Instrument) Timeline

Each state has its own timeline for mortgages. In states that use a mortgage instrument and judicial foreclosure, that timeline can vary enormously from as little as a few months to as much as a year more. Here's the typical timeline for Florida (135 days), one of the top states for foreclosures in the nation. *Note:* Check with the Florida real state department or with a Florida real estate attorney for the actual timelines, as they may vary, depending on your situation.

No matter how many threatening letters you receive from the lender, when you have a mortgage instrument, you're not in foreclosure until that lender issues a notice of default and records a notice of lis pendens with the local court. That gives notice that the lender is suing you for failure to make your mortgage payments. The foreclosure process has started. (*Note:* In Florida the lender is not required to notify you before beginning the foreclosure process, although your loan documents may require such notification.)

You then normally have 20 days (in Florida) to file an answer—namely, that you want to respond. Then a hearing is scheduled, and you have the opportunity to appear before a judge. In most cases the borrower does not choose to respond, and the judge rules in favor of the lender. However, if you decide to appear and actually have a good reason the foreclosure should not proceed, it may be halted. (A good reason may be that the lender has you confused with someone else, and you don't have a loan with this particular lender). In that case the judge may throw out the case. If you have an excuse, such as you lost your job, you've been or you are sick, and so on, the judge might give you more time.

If you're trying to sell your home on a short sale, you probably need as much time as possible. Therefore, it's usually to your advantage to request a hearing, because the courts are crowded these days, and it could take weeks, if not months, to schedule. During that time you could find a buyer and get the lender to agree to a short sale. Even if eventually you never appear at the hearing or appear with a lame excuse, you might have bought yourself enough time to slip out of foreclosure.

Keep in mind that your goal may not be to win the foreclosure suit. It may be simply to gain more time. A judge can postpone the hearing if, for example, you are too sick to attend on the scheduled day. Or if some other pressing matter occurs. Post-ponements can happen repeatedly.

Assuming you don't appear, the lender's attorney will typically request a summary judgment hearing. Again, delays are possible.

TRAP

In some areas of the country there is something called "sewer service." Here an unscrupulous server will throw the notice in the sewer yet swear that it was served. Thus, simply not being available may not always mean you won't be "served."

At a second hearing, the lender's attorney will present the case against you and, assuming it's valid in the judge's eyes, a foreclosure sale date will be set. This is when your home will be sold at public auction. It's usually at least 30 or more days later. Typically that's about three months from the time you were first notified of your default.

On the appointed day, your home will be sold. Usually, unless you have made prior arrangements with the lender to postpone the sale (as, for example, if you have a short sale in progress that the lender approves), your property will be auctioned on the courthouse steps.

Right of Redemption

You can redeem your house at any time prior to the auction by paying off the mortgage or, with the consent of the lender, making up all back payments. Also, it usually takes the court about 10 days to review the auction itself, and during that time you might also be able to redeem the property by paying off the mortgage in full. Be sure to check with an attorney about this.

If the judge approves the sale, the sheriff will be called. If you haven't already left the home, you will be evicted—your possessions will be put out into the street, and you will be barred from the home.

Deficiency Judgment

As noted earlier, if the judge approves the auction and the auction did not bring enough money to satisfy the mortgage, at the request of the lender after the auction a judgment might be entered against you for the deficiency. Once recorded, the lender could use this judgment to attach your other assets or, potentially, even to garnish your wages. (See the discussion in Chapter 2 on purchase money mortgages.)

Trust Deed Timeline

Here's the timeframe for the foreclosure process of a trust deed in California (120 days minimum), which is the model for about a third of the other states. California recently had the unfortunate honor of being the number one state in the union in foreclosures, although that dubious title is being challenged by Florida, Arizona, Nevada, and other states.

Once you stop making payments, the lender will begin sending you letters demanding payment and typically adding on a penalty plus additional interest. That can go on for anywhere from a month to a year or more, depending on the lender, how efficient its foreclosure department is, and how badly it wants to foreclose.

Along the way the lender will probably try to contact you (if you haven't already contacted the lender) and attempt to set up a meeting. This is called a "loan modification" meeting, and during it the lender will attempt to counsel you on how you might come up with the monthly payments.

Unfortunately, many loan modification meetings end up as a waste of time for the borrower, since they don't dramatically reduce the monthly payment, which is the one thing the borrower needs to have happen in order to stay afloat. (That is changing with the Obama mortgage modification program.)

After an attempt at loan modification (or sometimes before), if you continue to miss your monthly payments, eventually the lender will file a notice of default and will notify the trustee that holds a form of title to your property that you are officially in foreclosure. By recording this notice at the county recorder's office you (and anyone else who happens to be interested) are given formal notice that you're officially in foreclosure. The clock is ticking.

You now have three months (actually 90 days) at minimum in which to make good on all back payments, back interest, and penalties. In other words, you can redeem the loan at any time during the three-month period, and the lender has to take it out of foreclosure and put you back in good standing.

If you fail to do that (because you're upside down, don't have the money, can't sell, and so forth), the lender notifies the trustee to move forward with the foreclosure. The trustee then records a notice of trustee sale and advertises it in a "legal" paper. The borrower must receive a 20-day notice of the sale.

TIP A "legal" paper is any newspaper that publishes in your area. Don't expect the notice to be advertised in a major newspaper such as the *Los Angeles Times*, however. Most areas have tiny newspapers set up just to publish legal notices, and it will likely appear in one of those. Almost no one except investors and those involved in finance tend to read them.

During the advertising period, the lender no longer has to accept back payments, interest, and penalties. In other words, it can refuse to reinstate your loan. However, during this time you can still save the property by paying off the loan in its entirety. In others words, you can still pull off a short sale, *if* the lender is willing.

After the minimum period, your home is sold by the trustee on the "courthouse steps" to the highest bidder—in today's market that typically being the lender. Once the sale is completed, you have no further equity of redemption—you can't get your house back by paying off the lender.

Stopping the Foreclosure Process

Whether it's a mortgage or a trust deed, the processes we've seen can be halted at almost any point by the lender, if it chooses to do so. This can and does often occur when you've presented a short sale that the lender is willing to accept.

TRAP

Just be sure that someone in authority on the loan mitigation committee makes the phone call and sends the fax to the right person in the legal department so that the process is actually halted. Too many times a lender's left hand doesn't know what its right is doing and the foreclosure process marches on, even though a short sale is in the works.

Without a short sale, however, the process rolls on to the auction sale of your home. All of which is to say that you should find out what the deadlines are and make sure you do something before they occur.

Resources

To help you find out the timelines for your state, whether your state uses a judicial or non-judicial foreclosure, whether it uses a mortgage instrument or a trust deed, whether a deficiency judgment is allowed, and what the equity of redemption period, if any, is, check out the following Web sites (they often have the information posted under their various learning/education pages):

- www.foreclosure.com
- www.realtytrac.com
- www.foreclosureuniversity.com
- www.foreclosurelaw.org

Keep in mind, however that foreclosure laws change over time. To get the latest rules, check with your state's department of real estate and a good local attorney.

12

Alternatives You Should Consider

A short sale is one solution to the problem(s) you're facing when you're facing foreclosure, are under water, or are otherwise pressured to get rid of a home. There are, however, alternatives. In fact, one of these might be a better choice for you than a short sale.

This chapter covers several alternatives to a short sale that you might want to consider.

Deed in Lieu of Foreclosure

A deed in lieu of foreclosure became popular during the recession of the early 1990s, but it has not seen much of a resurgence lately. We'll see why.

Called simply a "deed in lieu," it's where the borrower deeds the property directly to the foreclosing lender. In exchange, the lender agrees to release the borrower from any further liability named in the loan agreements.

If you're going to pursue a deed in lieu, be sure you get a good attorney to help
you both with the documents you'll need and with negotiating with the lender.
If you're not careful, you could end up not owning the property but still have a
liability to a lender!

Note the big difference between a short sale and a deed in lieu.
In the former, there is an outside buyer for the property. The
lender merely agrees to take a short payoff. The outside buyer
then proceeds with the purchase. At the close of escrow not only
has the seller sold the property but the lender is also off the hook.
The discounted loan has been paid off. That's a big incentive to the
lender as well as the seller.

In a deed in lieu, there is no outside buyer. Rather, the lender
ends up owning the property, which it must now dispose of. One
of the big differences to a lender between a deed in lieu and foreclosure is time. The deed in lieu saves the lender the time it would
otherwise take to proceed with the foreclosure process. (Another
difference is that a formal foreclosure wipes out junior mortgages
and other liens on the property—if you deed it back to the lender,
however, there may still be other mortgages/liens that the lender
now has to deal with.)

The presumed advantage to a borrower is that there is no
foreclosure on his or her credit report. It's not there because it
never happened. The deed in lieu occurred and stopped the foreclosure process.

If you're a mortgage holder, don't celebrate yet, however.
Most lenders will report a deed in lieu to credit reporting agencies
who will put it into their credit reports. When new lenders see it
there, many consider it tantamount to a foreclosure. (It is, after
all, just advancing the foreclosure process.) Thus, very little may
be gained.

If you have a choice, a short sale is usually much more advantageous than a deed in lieu. With a short sale you may end up with

nothing more than a few missed payments on your credit report. A deed in lieu on that credit report, however, can be much worse.

Many sellers/mortgagors who are under water would like to do nothing better than to simply deed their property over to the lender. However, just because you deed it over doesn't mean that the lender has released you from your liabilities under the loan agreements you originally signed.

The lender could then take you to court, possibly get a judgment against you, and tie up your other assets and even garnish your wages. Simply giving the property to the lender doesn't usually work. (Remember, the lender didn't own it originally, so you're not really giving it "back.") The lender has to accept it and *release* you from liabilities.

Keep in mind that lenders don't want your property. They want your performing mortgage. When you perform on your mortgage (make your payments), it's considered an asset to a lender. When you fail to make payments, or you give it back to them (and it becomes an REO—real estate owned), it turns into a liability. Assets make profits; liabilities sink lenders.

Also, the lender may not be willing to accept the deed in lieu until you've gotten releases from junior mortgages and other lien holders.

However, if you decide that you want to pursue a deed in lieu, as with a short sale, you should first find out who's in charge. This is usually the loss mitigation committee or representative. (Loan modification officers rarely have the authority to receive a deed in lieu and release your liabilities.) See Chapter 6 for more details on finding the right person.

Then you must accomplish two things. The first is to demonstrate that you are going to lose the property to foreclosure to this lender.

Missed payments, being under water, and not having income and other assets will usually do the trick. Combine this with a hardship letter (such as is found in Chapter 8) and you can put together your own deed in lieu package. Remember, the whole point of this package is to convince the lender that foreclosure is inevitable. The lender may ask why you don't pursue a short sale, and you should be prepared with an answer. It's a good question—one I would ask you, too.

The reason you need to demonstrate hardship is to show the lender that you can't avoid foreclosure and convince it that there's no real reason to pursue you, since you don't have any other assets.

TRAP

Remember that as soon as the lender accepts the deed in lieu, you have to be out of the property. You can't deed it over to the lender and continue to live there (unless the lender gives you some sort of rental agreement, which would be unusual).

The second thing you need to accomplish is to convince the lender that accepting the deed in lieu makes good financial sense for it. You can point out that going through the foreclosure process could take many more months. (Be sure you know how long it will take in your state—see Chapter 11.) During that time the lender will accrue more lost interest. Further, since you're not going to be especially motivated to take care of the property (since you're losing it), there could be lots more deferred maintenance that the lender will need to correct before it can sell the property after foreclosure.

In short, you need to show the lender that it will save money by accepting your deed in lieu of foreclosure. If you do that, the lender may be willing to go forward with you.

TIP

Before you deed the property over, be sure you have fully worked out an arrangement in which the foreclosing lender (and other junior lenders as well) releases you of further liability. If a lender can still come after you once the deed is recorded, you've lost your leverage and possibly much more.

Bankruptcy

If you are insolvent, you can file for bankruptcy. These days individuals pretty much are limited to Chapter 13, which restructures your debt. Be sure to check with an attorney first before going forward with any bankruptcy.

As of this writing, unfortunately, bankruptcy judges do not have the power to change the terms or reduce the amount of a mortgage. (See Chapter 7 for possible changes, here.) Thus, while they may be able to help with your other debt, such as auto loans, credit cards and so forth, there's very little they can actually do with respect to the debt on your home.

Renting Out the Property

Sometimes a viable alternative that too few people who are under water and in financial trouble consider is renting out the property to raise money to make the mortgage payment. You can become a landlord.

Of course, it does involve your moving out and into another place (which you may rent or even buy). But, then, if you're facing foreclosure, you're going to have to move, or be evicted, anyhow.

Is Your Property in a Rentable Area?

Renting out the property works best in areas where there are a limited number of foreclosures. For example, in most parts of the country, although there are occasional foreclosures, the neighborhoods remain sound and there are people looking to rent in them. If this is your situation, you might want to consider renting as an alternative.

On the other hand, in some parts of the country (such as areas of southern Florida, central California, urban Nevada, and so on), virtually every house on a block is in foreclosure and vacant. Here it's very difficult to rent and probably would not be a viable alternative.

If your area is rentable, chances are that there are plenty of tenants looking. People who have been displaced by foreclosure need to live somewhere. And, often, once they've gotten rid of a property they couldn't afford through foreclosure, they make excellent tenants.

Can You Landlord?

Over the years I've rented out many properties and written books on the subject. Becoming a landlord is for some people, but not for everyone. For some folks, it's just unbearably aggravating. For others, it's a cakewalk.

Here are some tips to consider when making a decision on whether or not to rent out your home as an alternative to a short sale:

- **Can you make enough rental income to cover your payments?**
  It only makes sense to consider your property as a rental if it brings in a big enough income. Hopefully you'll get enough to cover PITI (principal, interest, taxes, and insurance). If you're far short of making that much, then renting out probably doesn't make much sense. You'd still be forced to take a lot of money each month out of your pocket to cover the difference.

- **Are there too many or too few rentals in your area?**
  Some areas are perfect for rentals. There's a strong tenant market and relatively few competing properties. In other areas, almost every house is for rent. Check your local newspaper for rental advertisements—a few is a good sign; page after page is bad. Check around your neighborhood for rental signs. It does not bode well if you see a lot of them. But a few signs suggest a good area for rentals.

- **How far away from the property will you move?**
  You never want to be more than half an hour by car away
  from your rental. (An hour is doable but far more difficult.)
  If you're close by, you can take care of renting it (finding
  tenants), quickly go over to the house when something
  breaks (like a faucet), and handle maintenance and other
  issues that crop up.

- **Are you willing to be a landlord?**
  There's more to being a landlord than meets the eye. You
  have to handle cleanup when tenants move out. You have to
  rush over when something breaks or needs repair. There's
  the potential problem of collecting rents when tenants fail to
  pay. And of course, in the worst case, there could be the need
  to evict a tenant. Being a landlord is no bowl of cherries.

- **Do you have the money to be a landlord?**
  It's going to take some start up money to handle a rental.
  You'll need cash to get the property ready, make payments
  while its vacant until you find tenants, pay any negative
  cash flow (see above), cover the costs of repairs and maintenance, and so on. If you're already behind on your mortgage payments and don't have the money to catch up,
  unless your home can be rented for a strong positive cash
  flow, you probably can't afford to rent it out.

There are many other issues involved in renting. But these are
some of the basics you need to consider. For more information,
consider a good book on renting. I recommend my own, *Buy, Rent,
And Sell*, McGraw-Hill, 2008.

Take on a Partner

Taking on partners was very popular a few years ago, but I haven't
seen much of it recently. Very likely that's because it only works if

you're right side up, or very close. If you're under water, you're not likely to find a partner.

Taking on a partner can be an alternative if your home is still worth at least as much as you owe. The whole idea here is that you'll give someone a piece of your action in the property (part ownership) in exchange for that person helping you make the payments. Later, when the real estate recession is over and prices move up again, you'll sell the property and split the profits.

I'm sure some readers are wondering, if the property is not under water, why not simply refinance instead of taking on a partner? Not everyone can refi. This is especially true if you have some temporary hardship, such as one member of your family has lost a job, and you've missed a few payments here and there and as a result your credit rating has plunged.

Yes, refinancing might be a better alternative, but only if it's available. A partner, however, sometimes can take up the slack when refinancing isn't possible.

Where Do I Find a Partner?

If you're wondering where you can find a partner, the fact is that you might already know one—a friend, a relative, or an associate. These make the best partners because you already know and, presumably, trust them.

TRAP

Don't take on a partner on a handshake. Whenever you take on a partner, no matter who, you need a written and signed partnership agreement. It should spell out what's involved and how any future profits or losses are handled. Make sure it's written by a good attorney so it will hold up if challenged.

If your partner is not someone you know, then you may need to advertise for an investor who wants to partner in real estate. However, if you do, be extremely careful of scam artists who are coming out of the woodwork these days, eager to scam away your house and your money. (See Chapter 13.)

What Will the Partner Do?

For an interest in your property, the partner may give you a one-time cash infusion, or a partner may pay a portion of the mortgage payment each month—for example, half.

Keep in mind, of course, that the partner eyes this as an investment. He or she isn't likely to be interested unless the cost of acquisition (getting in) is low and the chance of profit (selling later on) is high. That's why sometimes getting someone you know works best—this person might be willing to go along as a favor to you.

Alternatives

Whether it's giving a deed in lieu, renting, or taking on a partner, there are alternatives. Of course, each has its limitation. But they should be considered in your overall evaluation of whether or not to proceed with a short sale.

Scams to Avoid

I t seems that any time there's something new on the block, the scam artists come out of the woodwork to try to take advantage of it. In this case, scammers appear to have set their sights on sellers/mortgagors who want loan modifications or short sales.

There's no shortage of people out there ready to take advantage of you. This chapter covers a few of the many scams that have recently been going around.

Fixers and Facilitators

Fixers and facilitators are people who advertise that, for a fee, they can do for you what you can do for yourself. Essentially they claim to be able to fix things—help you negotiate a loan modification or a short sale.

Of course, there's nothing wrong with having expert help. A good attorney on your side is a decided advantage. A good real estate agent can make a short sale happen. I have no quarrel with such people.

Rather, my concern is with scammers who don't really provide a service, who sometimes make things worse, and who take your money. Here are some areas to watch out for:

1. **Beware when there is a demand for up-front money.** Once you've paid your money, it's too easy for the scammer to simply disappear, leaving you where you were before—but poorer. (Even if there are so-called guarantees of service, are you really going to track down the fixer who doesn't perform and then sue to recover your funds?) Of course, experts are legitimately entitled to a fee for service, or in the case of an agent, a commission. But, usually this comes at the back end, after service has been performed.

2. **Beware of someone who claims to be able to get your loan "fixed."** Loan modifications involve negotiating with a lender. Normally that's done directly by you. Of course, you could hire an attorney to go with you and give you expert advice—a good idea. Or you could hire an attorney to negotiate in your stead—not such a good idea. (If you were a lender, would you be inclined to modify a mort-gage for a borrower who didn't have time to show up her-self and who had the funds to hire an attorney in her place?) In any event, many loan modifications generally do not result in great "fixes." (See Chapter 7.)

3. **Be sure you understand the services offered.** Too often all that the fixer will do is fill in some forms, write a couple of letters, and perhaps make a phone call or two. For this you could be charged $1,000 or more. Of course, if it pro-duces a big loan modification that you're happy with,

you'd probably be thrilled to pay it. But, what if it produces nothing? You could still be charged for the service. Better to have an arrangement based on results, not on wheel spinning.

TRAP

The only person who can negotiate a *loan modification* with a lender is you, or someone you designate to go in your stead. An attorney can do this. Generally speaking, a real estate agent cannot—negotiating on behalf of someone else means legal representation, and a real estate agent does not have that power. Of course, you could give someone your "power of attorney," to negotiate for you. But then, you'd be committed to whatever that person came up with. (You should *not* give anyone your power of attorney before checking with a lawyer to learn the consequences.)

TIP

A real estate agent normally can present a *short sale* offer to a lender but cannot negotiate for you with that lender. I've heard it said that it's better to use an attorney to present your short sale offer. I'm not so sure. One attorney bragged to me that he would never have allowed the borrower in a deal to sign a promissory note for a portion of the discount on the loan. An agent commented that if the borrower hadn't signed the note, there wouldn't have been a short sale at all. Sometimes you can be overprotected.

Double Escrows

Double escrows are an old scam with a new twist. (They're also sometimes called "simultaneous closings.") It works like this: An unscrupulous real estate agent finds a buyer for your property for one price, say $300,000. He then uses a straw buyer, perhaps a relative of his, to come in with a lower price, say $270,000. He presents the $270,000 offer to you, the seller.

Since you don't really care what the price is—you only want out—you sign the lower offer. The real estate agent then presents the lower offer to the lender with a completed short sale package.

When the lender accepts, an escrow is opened, usually by the lender to facilitate the sale. At the same time, the agent opens a second escrow for the real buyer. Both escrows close simultaneously. In the first, the lender transfers the property to the straw buyer for $270,000. In the second the straw buyer transfers it to the real buyer for $300,000.

The agent pockets the $30,000 difference. Plus, the agent gets the commission on the $270,000 sale. The total is over $45,000. Not bad for a bit of sleight of hand.

Of course, the trouble is that it's fraud. If the lender finds out, it's going to be hopping mad and will probably come after you, the borrower, to make up that $30,000 difference, even if you're innocent. So you definitely want to avoid this.

How do you avoid this kind of scam? The best and sometimes only way is to deal only with a reputable real estate agent. (See Chapter 4 for help finding one.) No good agent would ever risk his or her license and livelihood, not to mention jail time, with such a scheme.

The Self-Help Bailout

There's a variation on the double escrow scheme that some unscrupulous sellers have attempted to pull off. It comes about because of the seller's desire to get a lower mortgage, given what's happened to the market around. After all, this seller argues, why should I keep paying on a $450,000 mortgage when my property is now worth only $300,000?

So the seller arranges with a relative, say an aunt with a different last name, to buy the property. This is the straw buyer. She buys it for $290,000. A short sale is arranged with the mortgage lender. Then, either as part of a double escrow as described above or shortly afterward, the aunt transfers the property back to the original seller in the form of an unrecorded deed. (It's not recorded so the lender doesn't find out.) The original seller makes the payments on the new loan through the aunt.

Now the seller has his cake and can eat it, too. He still owns the property, only he has a much lower loan on it. He's gotten the lender to eat the $150,000-plus that his home has dropped in value. Eventually, he refinances, pays off his aunt, and is home free, he hopes.

This is fraud. The reason is that a short sale transaction is presumed by the lender to be "arm's length." That means that there are no side deals or arrangements between family members of the seller, unless they are disclosed and the lender is aware this is happening and agrees to it. Of course, it's unlikely a lender would agree. It only agrees to the short sale because it presumes this is the best legitimate offer it's likely to get.

To avoid this problem, some lenders are now requiring sellers to sign an "occupancy agreement" as a condition of a short sale. It specifies that no close family member of the seller can occupy the property after the short sale. Some lenders even send someone by to see who's actually living in the home!

If the lender discovers the fraud, you can be sure it will be hopping mad and will come after the seller for the more than $150,000 it lost. Further, it could turn the whole matter over the FBI for criminal investigation.

All of which is to say, don't be even remotely tempted to try such a scam.

Phony Leasebacks

A phony leaseback is a tricky scam that's being played on some sellers who are under water and can't afford the payments on their mortgage. It's particularly onerous because it takes money from those who really can't afford to lose it. Here's how it works.

Someone comes by the house, or calls, or sends a mailer, and a desperate seller answers. The person who responds promises that he can resolve the seller's problems.

All the seller has to do is to *sign the house over* to this fixer. Usually a quitclaim deed has been prepared and is ready for the seller's signature, along with an authorization for the fixer to negotiate for the seller with her mortgage lender.

The seller is told that after she signs over her home, she can lease it back for a sum that she can afford each month. In the meantime the fixer will go to the lender and arrange for new financing so that she can keep the property.

Once that's all done, the fixer will deed the property back to the seller/mortgagor. She then will have a new, lower loan with lower payments, and she can then move forward still owning her home. It sounds too good to be true. And it is.

Here's what really happens. Once the seller agrees to transfer title to the fixer, there are two variations that play out. In the first, the fixer collects the lease money each month while negotiating with the lender for a short sale, getting as many extensions on the foreclosure as possible. Some fixers in this situation can get the process slowed down for many months, as much as a year or more. During all that time, the original seller is paying the fixer a monthly lease amount, which the fixer pockets.

Then, when no more extensions are possible, the fixer tells the sellers that he couldn't actually arrange a short sale. The house is going to auction. She and her family will have to move out. The poor seller, sometimes thanking the fixer for having tried his best, loses her home.

Of course, by not working with this fixer, the seller might have been able to legitimately short sell the home on her own or with the aid of a reputable agent. And she might thereby have saved her credit and eventually been able to purchase another home.

The second variation on this scam is when the fixer actually does negotiate a short sale either to a legitimate buyer or to a straw buyer as in the previous scam. If it is arranged, one day the fixer tells the seller that a short sale was arranged. She'll lose her home, but at least her credit won't be completely ruined. Again, the seller thanks the fixer for helping her out. In the meantime the scammer has pocketed all the rent money paid on the lease—and in some cases also gets a fee for service.

How do you avoid this scam? That's the easy part—don't sign your home over to someone else who promises to fix your mortgage financing. There's no need. You can negotiate directly with the lender yourself. Or you can authorize a competent person to negotiate for you. (See Chapter 6.) Signing over your home complicates, not simplifies, matters. And it may lead to a scam that can cost you money needlessly.

Phony Net Sheet

There are two kinds of net sheets used in short sales. The first is the PNS (preliminary net sheet) prepared for the seller. It shows how much the seller is likely to net from the house on a sale. Sellers use it to determine if they can do a traditional sale or refinance, or whether they need a short sale. (See Chapter 3.) While it is possible for it to be distorted, usually a seller will pretty much know if he or she is under water and owes more than the house is worth. If someone prepares a PNS for you, be sure you carefully analyze the figures on it to see that they are accurate. You don't want an unscrupulous person to force you into a short sale from which he or she may benefit and which you might not need.

The other net sheet is the one that's prepared for the lender. It shows the lender how much it will net from a short sale compared to how much it's net would be if it continues on with the foreclosure. (See Chapter 8.)

Here, sometimes an agent or a seller will exaggerate costs to justify a much lower short sale price. The reason is to get a quicker sale. The lower the price for the home, the sooner a buyer is likely to be found.

Costs for repair work are sometimes exaggerated. It might not require much arm twisting to get a roofer to give you an estimate saying that you need a new roof, not repair an old one. (A new roof can cost $10,000 or more, while repairs may run as little as a few hundred dollars.) Or that the house has an expensive structural problem, or a foundation problem, or whatever. These items can reduce the home's value by tens of thousands of dollars to the point where it becomes a bargain and a buyer can be quickly found. Of course, the buyer is informed that there's no work that really needs to be done and is happy to get the place at a reduced price.

If the repairs aren't really necessary, then the net sheet is presenting false information to the lender which, if it acts on it, might agree to a much lower short sale price than needed. Again, it's probably fraud.

Another problem area with a net sheet is the valuation of the property. In a falling market, just how much is a property really worth?

While the lender may ask for its own BPO, many agents and sellers will submit their own appraisal. If the appraisal is slanted downward and the lender accepts it, it could result in a lower-than-necessary short sale price.

The motivation in this case is to get the property sold quickly. While that's admirable from the seller's and agent's perspective, cheating the lender is no way to do it.

Other Scams

The scams discussed in this chapter are just a few of the short sale scams you should watch out for. Others pop up every day.

To avoid them, deal only with reputable agents and others. Think through any proposals given to you. Ask what the motivation is of people presenting offers to you. And consult with your attorney when in doubt.

And to quote the title of that old W. C. Fields movie, "You can't cheat an honest man."

Resources, Helpful Definitions, and Types of Mortgages

This chapter provides a variety of information you may find useful in your quest for a short sale.

Resources

Following are some Web sites you may find useful:

www.realestateradiousa.com

This site appears aimed squarely at real estate agents who want to learn more about the business. However, it has a section on short sales that is terrific for sellers (and buyers!).

Part of the short sale section includes an audiovisual presentation to help visitors to the site understand what a short sale is. It's very informative.

Another part of the site is devoted to investing in properties and includes a section of forms devoted to short sales. (Several of the forms used in this book are courtesy of this site.) You'll find just about every kind of real estate and short sale form you need. And best of all, as of this writing, they are downloadable for free. (The site also offers a complete short sale package of documents for $99.)

You may want to contact this site for aid in finding a real estate agent to help you with your short sale.

www.shortsale.org

Located in Southern California, this site has agents who specialize in handling short sales. The site contains a great deal of information. However, to really get the benefits the group offers, you need to call and speak to a representative.

On the site you can tune in to a video blog that explains a lot about short sales.

Reps emphasize that the organization's service is free to the seller. (It really is, since the agent's fee is, in effect, paid by the foreclosing lender who authorizes the short sale.)

The people at ShortSale.org handle the entire process with the lender. Says one rep: "We make the short sale process as painless as possible with a fast, efficient staff."

You can contact them at info@shortsale.org or call 888-885-5555.

www.shortsaleblogger.com

This is a blogging site run by Dave Peebles of Century 21 First Realty out of Florida.

The site is pretty much whatever Dave wants it to be. What makes it so interesting is that it's chock full of short sale information, including special areas for buyers, sellers, and agents.

Articles are from all areas of the media and are very timely and relevant. You'll find some of the latest information on short sales on this site.

In addition, Shortsaleblogger.com includes a host of well-written articles not only explaining how to handle a short sale but also giving useful tips on how to avoid or get around problems that are likely to occur. Dave's tips on what to include in your short sale package are particularly helpful. You can sign up for free postings.

Definitions of Terms Used in Short Sales

alt-A mortgage   A term that lenders use for mortgages that do not meet the strict standard underwriting guidelines for an A mortgage.

Traditionally if an A loan, for example, would require a credit score of 700 or higher, an alt-A might require a credit score of only 680 or even lower. (Scores in the 500s are generally considered to be subprime.)

After about 2000, however, alt-A loans also came to mean *low doc/no doc* loans. These are "stated" income/asset loans where little to no documentation is required to prove the borrowers income and assets. (See also *stated income/assets mortgage*.)

For some lenders alt-A loans have also come to mean loans that are subpar in some other area as well; for example, they do not have appropriate debt or loan-to-value (LTV) ratios or the property is not of the type usually found under standard underwriting. Thus an alt-A loan may mean the borrower has any or all of the following: lower credit score, little to no documentation to prove assets or income, an unqualified property, higher debt ratios, or lower LTV ratios.

The consequences of getting an alt-A loan are that it often carries a higher interest rate (meaning higher payments) and more onerous terms than an A grade mortgage.

authorization letter   A letter that the seller sends to the foreclosing lender authorizing it to talk with and disclose financial information and records to third parties. The letter is often addressed not just to the lender by company name but also to its attorneys, mortgage insurers, and servicers (another lender who may be charged with collecting mortgage payments and dealing directly with the borrower). Those who are authorized to receive information are usually mentioned by specific name such as ZYX Realty and Associates or Trustworthy Title Company. There may be a boilerplate sentence that allows the associates, agents, employees, and others who may be assigned by these companies to receive information as well.

The letter is signed by all borrowers on the mortgage, although not necessarily notarized. It's important that it be sent to a person in the foreclosing lender's company, not just generically to something like "Loss Mitigation Committee." A member of the committee, a loan negotiator, or a loan mediator in the company may well do. Usually your real estate agent and/or attorney will know to whom to address the letter. Without this letter of authorization, the lender normally will not release any of the borrower's financial information, and this could impede or even prevent a short sale.

Be wary of sending this letter, because it allows others to get your sensitive financial information. Check into Chapter 6.

BPO (broker's price opinion) This is a statement of opinion by a broker as to the value of a property. It is usually requested by a lender in lieu of a formal appraisal. The reason lenders prefer a BPO is that it can be done almost immediately, and the broker is typically paid a small sum (usually around $50) for the task, as opposed to an appraiser who would charge much more (typically $300 to $350). In a BPO the broker is usually asked to come up with three comparables (that is, homes very much like the subject home) that have sold in the past three months and three comparables that are currently offered for sale but have not yet sold. BPOs are used extensively by lenders to help establish current market value when a seller is asking for a short sale. Often a lender will base a decision to sell a property short (or not) on the BPO. Sometimes lenders will request two or more BPOs if they feel the property has been underappraised.

buyer's agent   A real estate agent who owes loyalty (fiduciary relationship) to the buyer. As a seller, you normally should not rely on this agent to give you advice that's in your best interest.

deed in lieu of foreclosure   An accelerated form of foreclosure that occurs when the borrower gets the lender to accept a deed to the property and stop the foreclosure process. It's important that the borrower get a full release from all lenders along with the deed in lieu, or else he or she could give up the property and still be liable for some debt. (See Chapter 12.)

default   When you are behind in your mortgage payments, you are said to be in default. Also, when the lender files a *notice of default*, it officially lets you know that you are behind in your payments and that the foreclosure process has begun. Even though you may be behind in your payments, in trust deed states you're technically not in foreclosure until a notice of default has been filed (i.e., recorded at the county or township's recording office). Once the notice of default has been filed, the clock begins ticking toward the ultimate auction of your property.

The timeframe is statutorily prescribed in each state. In California, for example, you have 90 days after the filing of a notice of default in which to make up all back payments (including penalties) in order to reinstate the mortgage. After the 90 days, you have an additional 21 days while a trustee advertises the auctioning of your property. During those 21 days you can save your property from being sold at auction by paying off the full amount of the mortgage At the end of that time, your property is irrevocably sold "on the courthouse steps" to the highest bidder, usually the lender. The important thing to note here is that *the notice of default* starts the whole foreclosure process.

deficiency judgment   A deficiency judgment is a court judgment that says that if the property does not yield enough money at a foreclosure auction to pay back the lender in full, then the borrower is personally responsible to make up any shortage, the deficiency. The judgment can be obtained as part of a judicial foreclosure through a mortgage instrument. If the foreclosure is non-judicial through a trust deed, the lender still will need to go to court to obtain the deficiency judgment. (Some states, such as California, do not allow a deficiency judgment if the property was foreclosed non-judicially or if the mortgage was part of the purchase price—"purchase money mortgage.")

The deficiency judgment, like other court judgments, will follow the borrower after the foreclosure and can be used to attach property and, in some cases, even garnish wages. As part of a short sale, the seller will usually demand that the lender waive any right to a deficiency judgment. Most lenders will agree because of the hardship to the borrower involved and to make the short sale deal. (Some states, such as Arizona, prohibit deficiency judgments.)

dual agent   A real estate agent who represents both the buyer and the seller in a transaction. (See Chapter 4.)

equity of redemption   The right a borrower has, after failing to make payments, to redeem his or her property by making up all amounts due on a mortgage, including back interest.

There are actually two types of equity of redemption. The first in effect occurs when the borrower can redeem—that is, put back into good standing—a mortgage that's in foreclosure. In other words, the borrower, by making up the amount owed in back payments and other interest, reinstates the loan, which then continues forward. The outstanding mortgage amount is still owed, the property is still in possession of the borrower, and future payments are due in a timely fashion.

ιe second type of equity of redemption occurs typically a foreclosure auction in which a borrower's property was to satisfy an unpaid mortgage debt. In some states, for a period of time after this auction, the borrower can still redeem the property, but not necessarily the mortgage, by paying the full amount owed back to the lender (or someone else) who bought it at auction. The borrower typically must pay this in cash, although the amount owed can be borrowed on the property from another lender. The original lender then no longer has a claim to the property. Time limits and deadlines are critical when exercising an equity of redemption.

financial statement   Also sometimes called an *income and expense statement* (see this term below). It typically will show all your assets and liabilities as well as your net worth. A lender will want to see your financial statement to be sure that you're not hiding assets that could be used to make payments on your mortgage. In the case of most borrowers, by the time they seek a short sale, their liabilities far exceed their assets.

forbearance   In a loan modification when the lender temporarily suspends payments. Usually, however, the missed payments must be made up later. Forbearance is sometimes granted in a loan modification when a borrower has a temporary problem, such as job loss or illness, but has good long-term prospects for being able to make the payments.

foreclosure   Most simply: when you don't make your mortgage payments and the lender sells your house to recoup the money it loaned. When you obtain a mortgage (or trust deed), you sign a contract that obligates you to meet many conditions, the most important of which is to make your payments on time. If you fail to make your payments (or break any other condition, such as failing to pay taxes on the property), the lender can either go to court (when a mortgage instrument is involved) or get a trustee sale (when a trust deed instrument is). After following procedures set out by each state to recoup the money originally loaned to you on the mortgage loan, the lender will have your home sold "on the courthouse steps." Typically the lender is the only bidder, and it takes possession. If necessary, the borrower is evicted from the premises by the local sheriff. See also *deficiency judgment* and *equity of redemption.*

hardship letter   A letter that goes to a lender in which the borrower explains why he or she cannot make the payments. (Also called an *excuse letter.*) This letter is an important part of the short sale package. The purpose of the letter is to demonstrate to a lender that the borrower cannot make the payments on the mortgage yet, because of extenuating circumstances, deserves a short sale. Typically the letter will list the financial, personal, medical, or other problems the borrower has as well as the various solutions he or she may have already tried, such as a loan modification. It may also list other alternatives that the borrower might pursue in the future, such as bankruptcy and a lawsuit to fight the foreclosure, but will forgo if the short sale is granted. It's important that this letter be clearly written, not be overly argumentative or threatening, and be a persuasive as possible. (See Chapter 8 for examples of hardship letters.)

income and expense statement   Use primarily for businesses, although they can be used for individuals. This statement shows your monthly and/or annual income and expenses. For an individual the expenses would usually include your mortgage payment(s), plus all other expenses from utilities to alimony. On the other side of the sheet is your income from all sources, including wages, commission, royalties, and so forth. Lenders often ask for an income and expense statement from self-employed individuals, seeking to get financing to see where those individuals are financially at a given time. For example, the lender may want 1040 statements for the previous few years and an income and expense statement for the current year (because taxes have not yet been filed).

lender   A financial institution or an individual who offers mortgages or other types of financing. Generically the term also may include a "servicer" who actually didn't make the mortgage but who is designated to receive payments and otherwise service the loan. A primary lender is usually an institution such as Wells Fargo or Countrywide that funds the mortgage. A secondary lender is an institution such as Fannie Mae or Freddie Mac that buys an aggregate of mortgages from a primary lender.

"liar's" loan   A mortgage in which there is no or little verification of the borrower's income or assets. Instead the borrower usually just states what the income and/or assets are, the lender obtains a credit report, and, assuming that the borrower has a sufficient credit score and the property appraises out, makes the loan. Nowadays, so-called liar's loans are seldom, if ever, made. See also *stated income/assets mortgage*.

loan modification committee   A lender's committee or representative authorized to work out problems with a borrower on a mortgage. (Also called a *workout department*.) The borrower who may be behind by several payments typically seeks to have them reduced. The lender tries to find ways to allow the borrower to get current on the mortgage and continue making payments. The loan modification committees were probably the biggest single disappointment of the recent mortgage crisis. Too seldom did their actions result in saving a borrower from foreclosure. Too often the loan modification committee was powerless to dramatically cut an interest rate or reduce a mortgage balance, the two things that would have greatly reduced payments. Rather, often the committee would forgive a few back payments, postpone payments, or extend the term of the mortgage, all of which did little to cut payments that

had sometimes reset to as much as twice or more of their original amount. (See also Chapter 7.)

BEWARE

Some private companies are claiming to offer loan modification for an up-
front fee. Then too often, they take the money and provide little or no service. It takes a lender to modify a mortgage (or, as may be the case if the
government passes new legislation, a bankruptcy judge). Be sure to check
out any loan modification company with the Better Business Bureau and
even your lender.

loan servicer   The one responsible for collecting loan payments,
handling escrow accounts, and communicating with the borrower, but which does not own the mortgage. Some major
lenders handle servicing as a way of augmenting their lending
business. The servicer may have no authority to handle a short
sale. (Also called a *lender.*)

loss mitigation committee   As the name suggests, this group,
organized by the lender, tries to mitigate or reduce losses from
bad mortgages. Usually the loss mitigation committee has the
authority to approve a short sale, if a complete package of documents is provided by the seller (or his or her agent). The loss
mitigation committee or work-out department for your lender
usually can be reached by calling the main phone number and
then working your way through the system until you find the
right contact. (For more information see Chapter 6.)

mortgage broker   An individual or a company that secures mortgages for a borrower from a lender. The mortgage broker typically works with many lenders and can offer the borrower a
range of options for interest rate, terms, and conditions of the
mortgage. When you fill out an application and other paperwork with a mortgage broker, it transmits it to the lender who
then makes the decision whether to make the loan or not. The
mortgage broker does not lend its own money. A mortgage
"banker" fulfills much of the same functions as a "broker," but

lends its own funds. The mortgage broker is paid an origina-
tion fee, often from the borrower, or a yield spread premium
(where the yield on the mortgage is adjusted to accommodate
the mortgage broker's fee) from the lender.

mortgage forgiveness debt relief act of 2007   This act works to
relieve sellers of short sales on their principle residences from
having the amount that their mortgage was discounted (or forgiven) considered as taxable income by the IRS. For example, if
the lender forgave $100,000 on the mortgage (discounted it by
that amount) in order to facilitate a sale, it would report this to
the IRS and send the homeowner a 1099-C that showed it as
income. The homeowner then might need to pay taxes on the
forgiven amount.

The act amends the Internal Revenue Code and thus excludes
from a taxpayer's gross income such a discharge of indebtedness
when the mortgage was incurred to acquire a principle residence.
The exclusion was originally limited to the tax years 2007 to 2009,
but was extended to 2012. It also has a number of conditions and
limitations (such as a maximum exclusion of $2 million for mar-
ried couples filing jointly, $1 million for those filing separately).
So be sure to check with a Certified Public Accountant or tax spe-
cialist to see how it might effect you. (See also Chapter 10.)

no doc/low doc loans   A no doc loan means that the borrower
does not have to fill out most documentation to prove income
or assets. [Also sometimes called *NINA loans* (for *no income/no
assest*).] All that's required is that a short application form be
filled out giving personal information and, typically, the address
of the home being purchased. The lender pulls a credit report
and gets a credit score and appraisal and may verify the borrower's employment. These types of loans were popular during
the period of 2000 to 2006, although more recently, because of
the banking crisis, lenders have in general refused to issue them.
(Also sometimes called *alt-A mortgages* and *stated loans*.)

A low doc loan means that the borrower has to fill out minimum documentation—much less than with a traditional mortgage. An application is provided, and a credit report and credit score are pulled on the borrower. Then an appraisal is made of the property to determine the LTV (loan-to-value) ratio. Because little to no documentation is required to prove assets and/or income, the temptation is to exaggerate or outright lie on the application. Thus these became known as "liar's" loans.

No doc/low doc loans were particularly popular among entrepreneurs and the self-employed who may have had difficulty in verifying their true income, that is, income that was in the form of cash (that is, "under the table" and not reported). Such a borrower might have enough income to afford a big mortgage but is not able to document it, hence the value of low doc/no doc loans.

Because these loans obviously pose greater risks to the lender, they often came with higher interest rates and demands for larger down payments. During the collapse of the real estate market after 2006, it was discovered that many, if not most, of these mortgages were given to borrowers who in truth did not have enough income to qualify for the loan.

option ARM   An ARM (adjustable rate mortgage) in which the payments may vary at the option of the borrower (seldom used anymore). The payment option (for which the loan is named) usually allows the borrower, at his or her option, to pay a full monthly payment (interest and principal), pay interest only, or pay an amount less than the interest owed (similar to a teaser rate).

At one time these mortgages often were issued at 100 percent of loan-to-value (that is, nothing down) and came with a very attractive low-interest teaser. For example, while the market interest rate might be 6 percent, the initial interest rate for the first three years might be only 2 or 3 percent or less. The result was a greatly reduced payment, at first.

However, the teaser and payment option typically have ended after two or three years. At that time the loan resets to market rate (or higher, to make up for previously lost interest), and the payments jump up. Furthermore, any unpaid interest is added to the principal, so the loan grows over time (negative amortization).

During the period of 2005 to 2007, reports suggest that mortgage brokers were sometimes paid more to place buyers in option ARMs than other products. Lenders liked the option payment ARMs because many could claim the full monthly payment as revenue, whether paid by the borrower or not. And since these loans were sold and resold in the secondary market, often a distant financial institution such as a hedge fund might actually be setting the rates and terms and not the primary lender.

When these loans began to reset in 2008 to much higher payments, borrowers who could not refinance or resell because they were under water were often forced into foreclosure and began looking to short sell their properties.

paycheck/unemployment check stubs   This is the attached piece of paper (stub) you tear off before cashing your check. It usually gives the date, the issuer, the payee, and the amount. When preparing a short sale package that is to go to the lender, you can use it to document the amount you received.

performing mortgage   A mortgage in which the mortgagor (borrower) is keeping the payments current. This is as opposed to a *nonperforming* mortgage in which the borrower is behind in payments. A performing mortgage is considered an asset by lenders. A nonperforming mortgage, depending on how much in default the borrower is, may be considered a liability.

prime mortgage   Also called an *A mortgage*. This is considered a top-quality mortgage and must meet the underwriting standards of Freddie Mac and Fannie Mae. Such a mortgage is typically securitized and sold (and bought) on the secondary market. Generally speaking, today a credit score of 700 or higher and a debt ratio of no more than about 30 percent is required to get a prime mortgage. See also *subprime mortgage*.

reset   A feature of a balloon mortgage. It's when the interest rate on a mortgage changes, usually to a much higher rate. With an ARM (adjustable rate mortgage), a teaser may provide a low interest rate for a fixed period of time, often two or three years. Then, at the end of that period, the loan "resets" to a much higher rate. A reset is a feature of any mortgage with a low teaser rate.

sale/purchase agreement   The contract used to buy and sell a home. Also called a *deposit receipt*. It normally specifies the price, the property, the buyers and sellers, the deposit, the down payment, and all the terms and conditions of the sale. It is the document used to open an escrow account. It is not valid unless and until the buyer and the seller both have signed an identical version of it. When the buyer, the seller, or other parties (such as an agent) have a question concerning how some element of a sale is to be handled, they usually refer back to the sale/purchase agreement.

seller's agent   An agent who owes loyalty (that is, fiduciary relationship) to the seller. Normally the agent who lists your home is the seller's agent, and you can rely on his or her loyalty. However, if that agent then finds a buyer, he or she may become a "dual agent," representing both. An agent must give you a written statement of whom he or she represents. As a buyer, you normally should not rely on a seller's agent to give you advice that's in your best interest.

short payoff proposal (to lender)   A brief description of the essence of the short sale that tells the lender what its net is going to be. Sometimes a HUD-1 or a lender net sheet is used as a short payoff proposal. It's an important part of a short sale package presented to the lender. (See Chapter 8.)

short sale   When you owe more on your property than it is worth, you're considered under water or upside down. If you then sell that property and the lender accepts less than it's owed in order to make the deal, it's a short sale or, as it's also sometimes called, a *short payoff*. Short sales are common when the market is down and housing prices have fallen. They are very rare when the market is up and housing prices are rising.

short sale package   The package that is sent to the mortgage lender that contains all the documents necessary for that lender to reach a decision on a short sale. The package may be prepared by the agent or the seller. It typically contains a proposal letter, a hardship letter, documentation, and other information that the lender requires. Every lender may have its own requirements, so be sure to contact your lender before sending in the package. (See Chapter 8.)

stated income/assets mortgage   In a stated income/assets loan, the borrower only has to "state" what his or her income and assets are in order to qualify. The borrower does not have to verify that income through documentation, as would be the case with a traditional mortgage. The lender, however, will normally obtain a credit report and credit score and will verify the employment of the borrower and may ask to see a breakdown of the borrower's debt. These loans usually carry with them higher interest rates and larger down payment requirements. These are sometimes broken down into separate categories—stated income and stated assets.

In a *stated income loan* the borrower's income is simply stated and not documented. The lender may, however, require that the borrower prove assets and list debts. Self-employed people who may have unreported cash income typically find this type of financing appealing, although it usually carries a stiffer interest rate and requires a bigger down payment. Since about 2006, when many of these types of loans went into default, lenders have in general refused to issue them. (Also sometimes called a *no income verification loan*.)

A stated asset loan requires the borrower to state, but not document, assets. These include money in demand deposits, stock, and other real estate. The borrower must still, however, document income and show a good credit report and credit score. As with stated income loans, this type of financing usually carries a stiffer interest rate and requires a bigger down payment. Since about 2006, when many of these types of loans went into default, lenders have in general refused to issue them. (See also *no doc/lo doc loans* and *"liar's" loans*.)

subprime mortgage Sometimes called a *B mortgage*. A mortgage offered to borrowers who have impaired credit or little to no credit history—borrowers who represent an increased risk to lenders and hence who cannot qualify for a prime (A) mortgage.

A decade ago this type of borrower simply could not get a mortgage. Then, during the housing bubble, lenders using complex computer models made loans (usually ARMs with little to no money down and big teasers) to subprime borrowers. They justified the risk of these loans by charging higher interest rates than they charged for prime mortgages. Because of the higher interest rates, they were considered desirable investments and were frequently bought on the secondary market by institutional lenders worldwide.

When the housing market crashed, the first fallout was the subprime borrowers, many of whose ARMs reset to higher interest rates and payments than they could afford. This had a ripple effect throughout the banking industry and brought down many financial institutions that had bought these loans. As of this writing, subprime mortgages are generally unavailable.

taxable income on short sale loss When the seller reports the amount of its loss or discount on a short sale to the IRS as income to the borrower/seller of the property. Sometimes this income may be considered taxable. A good accountant or tax attorney should be consulted before a borrower undertakes a short sale to determine the tax consequences of the sale. (See Chapter 10.)

tax return   A document filed with a taxing authority, such as the Internal Revenue Service or the State Franchise Tax Board, that states the payer's tax liability as well as the amount of tax paid. A common tax return is the 1040 filed with the IRS. That document is often required when a mortgage or a short sale is being processed.

teaser   An incentive interest rate offered during the initial terms of a mortgage. A low introductory rate. Most ARMs (adjustable rate mortgages) will offer a teaser to entice borrowers to get the loan. Teaser rates can be for as short as a month or for as long as three years or more. For example, a loan may carry a rate at the current interest market of 6 percent. However, for the first three years of the loan, that rate is reduced to 3 percent as an incentive to the borrower to take out the financing.

It is important to understand that the amount of interest the lender "loses" as part of the teaser is in actuality rarely lost. It may be recouped by the lender charging a higher-than-market interest rate once the teaser expires. Or it may be recouped by taking the interest not paid and adding it to the principal of the mortgage (negative amortization). When the teaser expires, the mortgage typically resets to a higher interest rate and payment requirement.

In an upward-moving real estate market, borrowers are sometimes encouraged to take out ARMs with big teasers to get the benefits of a low initial payment. Then, it is suggested that when the teaser expires, they either sell the property or pay off the mortgage and get another with another low teaser. In downward-moving real estate markets, the ability to do this sort of sale or refinance is usually inhibited by falling prices, and borrowers may be stuck with the reset loan payments. This sometimes leads to foreclosure.

"walking" Abandoning a property—not making payments on a mortgage and leaving the property. The results of "walking" are normally foreclosure by the lender, which is usually added as a negative item to the borrower's credit report.

Types of Mortgages

Short sales are a solution, but not a panacea. They may not cure all your problems. And a lot depends on what type of mortgage you have.

There are different mortgage types. The two types of mortgage instruments commonly used in the United States are the *mortgage* (the term "mortgage" has come to generically mean all loans on homes as well as a specific financial instrument) and the *deed of trust.*

> **TIP**
>
> To find out whether you have a *trust deed* or a *mortgage*, check the loan documents you got when you bought or refinanced your property. If the documents talk about a *mortgagor* (borrower) and a *mortgagee* (lender), you've probably got a mortgage instrument. If they talk about a *trustor* (borrower), *beneficiary* (lender), and *trustee* (stakeholder), then you've got a deed of trust.

If You Have a Mortgage Instrument

There are two really important things to remember if you have a mortgage (as opposed to a trust deed). The first is that in order to foreclose, the lender must go to court. There is no non-judicial foreclosure on a mortgage instrument. This means that you will be able to appear and plead your case before a judge in a court of law.

Tell It to the Judge

Of course, courts tend to move through foreclosures rather quickly, and usually they tend to believe whatever the lender tells them. But, if you show up (very few borrowers actually do) and say something such as, "I mailed my payment checks on time, but the lender refused to accept them" (assuming it's true), the judge is likely to listen, particularly if you've got documentation to prove it. If you have another serious excuse such as you're pregnant or sick, and, even though you can't make the payments, you can demonstrate that you can't safely be moved from the house (presumably someone else would make this argument for you), the judge might also listen. Either way, while (as of this writing) the judge may not have the power to forgive the mortgage or even reduce the payments, he or she often does have the power to delay the foreclosure process.

Deficiency Judgment

The other important thing to remember is that when the lender goes to court (as opposed to non-judicial foreclosure), it can demand a *deficiency judgment* as part of the foreclosure process. A deficiency judgment essentially says that if the property does not yield enough money at a foreclosure auction to pay back the lender in full, then you are personally responsible to make up the deficiency. In other words any losses by the lender could come back to haunt you for years to come.

TIP

Some states have *purchase money laws* that prohibit a lender from securing a deficiency judgment on a mortgage that was issued as part of the purchase price of the property. Check the Web sites noted at the end of Chapter 11 to see if that includes your state. Purchase money mortgages do not apply to refinanced loans.

Few lenders seek a deficiency judgment as a matter of course for every foreclosure. Most bother only if they think that you, the borrower, have enough other assets and income to make it worthwhile. It's kind of a roll of the dice as to whether or not one will be filed against you as part of your mortgage's judicial foreclosure process.

If You Have a Trust Deed

A trust deed instrument is an entirely different kind of animal from a mortgage. It was invented largely out of necessity. Lenders were dissatisfied with the judicial process of the mortgage instrument, which could be delayed time and again by the borrower (mortgagor) appearing in court and pleading to a judge. The lenders wanted a way to foreclose *without* having to go to court.

What they came up with, beginning in California and then spreading to most states, was an instrument that did just that. When you obtained the loan, you signed documents that gave an independent third party control over the title to your home. This independent third party was called a *trustee*. It performed essentially the same function as a stakeholder in a bet. It held onto the title to your home. (This job is usually performed by a title insurance company or some other entity licensed to handle trust deeds.)

As long as you made your payments, the trustee did nothing. However, if the lender (called the "beneficiary") informed the trustee that you (being the trustor) had stopped making payments, the trustee would then sell your home (whose title it possessed) to the highest bidder on the courthouse steps. Over time, the entire process was codified in each state in which it is used.

No Judge to Tell It To

The big advantage of a trust deed for the lender (and disadvantage for you) is that the entire process could be moved forward quickly. And no appeal would be made by the borrower to a judge, because no court would be involved. Once started, the process ground on inexorably toward the final trustee auction of your property on the courthouse steps. In fact, should there be a mistake (for example, the lender or the trustee foreclosing on the wrong person and the wrong loan), the only way to stop the process (assuming you can't get the lender—beneficiary—to listen to reason) would be to go to court yourself. You'd have to initiate the action and probably end up paying the court costs. For the lender it was quick and easy.

On the other hand, not all the advantages favored the lender. Since no judicial action was involved, there could be no deficiency judgment. (No court—no judgment.) This means that if the property didn't bring enough at the auction to pay off the loan, even assuming it wasn't a purchase money mortgage noted earlier, you couldn't be held liable for the balance.

Of course, lenders today normally include a clause in the loan documents that you sign that gives them the opportunity, at their option, to foreclose judicially. If they want, they can go to court and can get a deficiency judgment against you (unless, as noted, the loan was a purchase money mortgage).

Most lenders, however, waive this right in order to get on with things more quickly by non-judicially foreclosing on the trust deed. However, if the lender believes that you have lots of assets and/or income, in some states it could, at its option, still go the judicial route and obtain that deficiency judgment.

TRAP

Although lenders may not have the legal right to a deficiency judgment in a non-judicial foreclosure, many will insist on a deficiency payment as a condition of granting a short sale. As part of the short sale agreement, they will demand that you sign a promissory note agreeing to pay them a certain amount of money over time. If you don't agree to the note, they don't agree to give you a short sale. They have the leverage, and most sellers will go along. Fortunately, the promissory note is typically for just a fraction of the amount of the loan that's forgiven.

Index